Number Two

Chicago Directory

1839

JUST ISSUED.

AN

HISTORICAL SKETCH

OF THE

EARLY MOVEMENT IN ILLINOIS FOR THE LEGALIZATION OF SLAVERY,

READ AT THE ANNUAL MEETING OF THE

CHICAGO HISTORICAL SOCIETY,

DECEMBER 5TH, 1864,

BY

HON. WILLIAM H. BROWN,

(Ex-President of the Society.)

"Et Patribus et Posteris."

CHICAGO:
FERGUS PRINTING COMPANY,
244 ILLINOIS STREET,
1876.

Yours sincerely
Robert Fergus.

Fergus'
DIRECTORY *of the*

City of Chicago

1839

WITH CITY AND COUNTY OFFICERS, CHURCHES, PUBLIC
BUILDINGS, HOTELS, ETC., ALSO, LIST OF SHERIFFS
OF COOK COUNTY AND MAYORS OF THE
CITY SINCE THEIR ORGANIZATION

TOGETHER WITH
POLL-LIST OF THE FIRST CITY ELECTION (TUESDAY, MAY 2, 1837) AND ALSO LIST OF PURCHASERS OF
LOTS IN THE FORT DEARBORN ADDITION, THE NO. OF LOTS, AND THE PRICE PAID, 1839; ETC., ETC.

Compiled by
Robert Fergus

HERITAGE BOOKS
2019

HERITAGE BOOKS

AN IMPRINT OF HERITAGE BOOKS, INC.

Books, CDs, and more—Worldwide

For our listing of thousands of titles see our website
at
www.HeritageBooks.com

A Facsimile Reprint
Published 2019 by
HERITAGE BOOKS, INC.
Publishing Division
5810 Ruatan Street
Berwyn Heights, Md. 20740

Entered according to Act of Congress, in the year 1876, by
Fergus Printing Company,
In the office of the Librarian of Congress, at Washington, D.C.

Originally published:
Fergus Printing Company,
244-8 Illinois Street, Chicago
1876

International Standard Book Numbers
Paperbound: 978-0-7884-3014-5
Clothbound: 978-0-7884-7591-7

INTRODUCTION.

We have no apology to offer in presenting a Directory thirty-six years after its original date. The new settler will see no use for it, but the "Old Settler" can read and refer to it with pleasure. It is hoped that the parties named in this work will never feel ashamed of the days when they earned an honest living "by the sweat of their brow."

> "Honor and shame from no condition rise;
> Act well your part—there all the honor lies."

In September, 1839, the Common Council ordered the revision and printing, in pamphlet form, of the Laws and Ordinances of the City. The work was tendered to Messrs. Rudd & Childs, printers, but they, not being able to find sufficient funds, offered to transfer the contract to the subscriber, who accepted and fulfilled it. There were six blank pages at the end, and Mr. Childs suggested the filling of them up with the names of the business men of the City, which was immediately done; no canvass was necessary, and the names were never written—each name, as thought of, was forthwith set up by the subscriber, until the six pages were completed. It never was supposed that the names of all the business men of the City were included in this list, but the necessary pages were filled up, and the title given those names the "CHICAGO BUSINESS DIRECTORY." There were no numbers on any street (except Lake Street,) at that time—the numbers now given are those of the present day.

On the completion of the Laws and Ordinances, fifty copies were delivered to the City, and the sum of $25.00 was ordered paid, January 27th, 1840. (See Common Council Proceedings, published in the *Daily Chicago American*, Jan. 2, and 29, and February 22, 1840.)*

"CORPORATION PRINTING.
"Robert Fergus,................... $25.00."

---

* See City Treasurer's Quarterly Report for January, February, and March, 1840. See, also, Common Council Proceedings, (in City Clerk's Office,) dated Feb. 20, 1840.

About fifty copies were sold to the citizens at fifty cents per copy; the balance of the 500 were never used in public.

This "*Chicago Business Directory*" was reprinted last year in pamphlet form, and a *fancy* history given to it. The subscriber began to complete the *Directory*, commenced in 1839, some two years ago, and can now say that our "Old Settlers" pronounce it complete. Had there not been incorrect statements made, by interested parties, perhaps this DIRECTORY never would have been printed; like the original, this never was canvassed for, or even written.

The *first* Directory of this City was carelessly canvassed for by James Wellington Norris, attorney, in the latter part of 1843. It was printed and published by William Ellis and Robert Fergus. The publishers had no trouble about the division of the profits of that speculation. Norris compiled three or four similar works in the years following, and, perhaps, with greater profit to all concerned.

The present publisher has since had some experience in Directories in this City. In 1854, 1855, and 1856 he again tried to place the Directory before the citizens in an improved form, but, unfortunately, his connections were not trustworthy, and, after considerable loss, he retired from the business.

In the compilation of this Directory, much assistance has been rendered by many of our old and intelligent citizens, for which the compiler returns sincere thanks.

This work has the sanction of Hon. John Wentworth, Hon. Julian S. Rumsey, Hon. Buckner S. Morris, Hon. Mahlon D. Ogden, James H. Rees, Esq., Joseph H. Gray, Esq., James A. Marshall, Esq., J. K. Botsford, Esq., Asahel Pierce, Esq., Peter Graff, Esq., Bennett Bailey, Esq., P. R. Morgan, Esq., and many other intelligent citizens, whose recollections of the days of 1839 are still bright.

ROBERT FERGUS.

FEBRUARY 1, 1876.

☞ The Publishers will be pleased to receive any names that have been omitted, or any mistakes that may have occurred.

Such additions or changes will be printed and furnished to purchasers of this Directory without charge.

FERGUS'
CHICAGO DIRECTORY,
1839.

Abbott, S. S., teamster, bds John Gray
Abel, Ralph, clerk, post-office, 37 Clark street
Abel, Sidney, Postmaster, office 37 Clark st
Achers, Simon, st. sub-contractor, Legg st. near Lill's brewery
Adams, George, butcher,
Adams, William, carpenter,
Adams, Wm. H., surveying, mapping, etc., Lake street
Adams & Co., Wm. H., boot and shoe dealers, 138 Lake street
Adsit, James M., carpenter, Monroe street, near Dearborn
Aiken, Samuel, shoemaker, Sangamon street
Albee, Cyrus P., butcher, Funk's market, cor. Lake & Dearborn
Allen, D. W. C., constable, bds Chicago Hotel.
Allen, Daniel, carpenter and joiner
Allen, Edward R., druggist, Leroy M. Boyce
Allen, Capt. James, steamboat builder, bds Lake House
Allen, James P., lumber dealer, So. Water st, foot of Franklin
Allen, John P., boot and shoemaker, North Water street
Allen, William, saloon, North Canal street south of Kinzie
Allison, Robert, house carpenter, Pine street near Michigan
Anderson, Asle, musician, North State street
Anderson, Endre, laborer, North State street
Anderson, Eric, pressman, North State street
Andrews, David, tailor, north side
Andrews, William, tailor, north side
Andrus & Doyle, grocery and provisions, South Water st
Andrus, Loomis, Andrus & Doyle,
Armstrong, Thomas, clerk, Gurdon S. Hubbard & Co.
Armstrong, William, clerk, G. S. Hubbard & Co.
Arnold, Isaac N., attorney and counsellor at law, Clark street
Arnold, J. M., carpenter, Madison street, 2d ward
Archdale, John, contractor, s.-west cor. Randolph and LaSalle
Archdale, jr., John, contractor, bds. John Archdale
Atwood, J. M., house, sign, and ornamental painter, Randolph
Austin, Dr. Wm. H., Dodge & Austin, Lake street
Avery, Charles E., lumber dealer, cor. LaSalle and So. Water
Avery, William, canal contractor, bds Lake House
Avery & Larrabee, commission merchants, South Water street
Ayres (Mahlon) & Iliff, dry goods, groceries, etc., Lake street

Bailey, Bennett, carpenter and builder
Bailey, Henry, house mover, with Chester Tupper
Bailey, Amos, carpenter and surveyor
Bailey, Joseph, carpenter,
Baimbridge, George, teamster, Chicago ave. near Cass street
Baker, Asahel, carpenter,
Baker, Franklin, clerk,
Baker, Hiram, attorney and real estate agent .
Baker, Perry, capitalist, bds. Michigan ave.
Baldwin, Wm. A., canal contractor, bds Tremont House
Ball, Lebbus, steamboat runner
Ballantine, David, canal contractor
Balestier, Joseph N., attorney and counsellor at law, 24 Clark st
Ballingall, Patrick, attorney at law, Lake st
Bancroft, J. W. & Co., Lake Street Coffee House, 135-7 Lake st
Bandle, Willis, blacksmith, Asahel Pierce
Bannon, Andrew, boarding house, cor. Randolph and Franklin
Barber, Jabez, lumber merchant, Market street near Randolph
Barnes, Hamilton, carpenter, West Madison street
Barnum, Truman, teamster, North Dearborn street cor. Indiana
Bartell, Thomas, saloon,
Barth, Nicholas, saloon and boarding-house, Randolph street
Bascom, Rev. Flavel, pastor First Presbyterian Church
Basset, George, hostler, City Hotel stables
Batcheller, Ezra, clerk, Mosely & McCord
Bates (A. S.) & Morgan (Caleb), cabinet makers and under-
 takers, 199 Lake st
Bates, Mrs. A. S., milliner, Wells st near Lake
Bates, jr., John, auctioneer, Lake street
Bates, Jacob R., clerk, Mansion House
Bates, ———, plasterer, bds "Rat's-castle"
Baumgarten, Charles, carpenter, Illinois street near North State
Baumgarten, Christopher, carpenter, Illinois street nr. N. State
Baumgarten, John, clerk, bds. Illinois street near North State
Baumgarten, Morris, Illinois street, near North State
Baumgarten, jr., Morris, carpenter, Illinois street near N. State
Bay, Jean Baptiste, laborer, Randolph st alley, near Fifth ave
Bay, Joseph, laborer, Randolph street alley, near Fifth ave
Beach, John, canal contractor, Randolph st, east of Dearborn
Bazley, Caleb, merchant and contractor, So. Water nr LaSalle
Beach, James S., printer, with E. H. Rudd
Beach, Oscar L., County Clerk's office
Beardsley, Capt., schooner Constitution
Beaubien, Charles H., violinist
Beaubien, John B., Michigan ave., bet. Lake and So. Water sts
Beaubien, Mark, hotel-keeper, Lake st
Beaubien, Medard B., merchant, South Water street
Beaumont (Geo. A. O.) & Skinner (Mark), attorneys and coun-
 sellors at law, Clark st cor. Lake
Bebb, Maurice, teamster, Wm. Lill
Beecher, Jerome, boot, shoe, and leather dealer, 160 Lake st
Beers, Cyrenus, Botsford & Beers
Beidler, Jacob, lumber merchant,
Bell, James, landscape gardener, 4th ward

Bennett, Henry, speculator, bds Illinois Exchange
Bennett, Samuel C., school-teacher, State street, cor. Madison
Bennett, Mary, assistant S. C. Bennett
Bennett, William, soap boiler
Benthune, Antoine, Parisian dyer, N. Water st. nr N. Dearborn
Benton, Lewis, speculator
Berdel, Nicholas, musician, Washington st
Berg, Adam, boarding-house, LaSalle st, near Lake
Berg, Anton, teamster,
Berg, Henry, teamster,
Berg, John, drayman,
Berg, Joseph, saddle and harness maker, Chas. E. Peck
Berkinbile, Christian Henry, carpenter, Government works
Berry, B. A. & Co., dry goods and grocery store, So. Water st
Berry, Francis, carpenter,
Bething, Antoine, dyer and scourer, North Water street
Betts, Dr. J. T., residence and office, Michigan st.
Bickerdike, George, farmer, West Indiana st
Bingham, Chas. K., Frink, Bingham & Co., 123 Lake street
Bishop, James E., canal contractor, Illinois street
Bishop, Thomas, bookkeeper, Philo Carpenter
Bishop, Thomas, farmer,
Bigelow, Henry W., dry goods, powder, etc., 136 Lake st
Bigelow, Liberty, lottery ticket dealer, 150½ Lake street
Bird, Edward, contractor, bds. J. Outhet
Black, Francis, auctioneer, Stanton & Black
Blackie, Andrew, stair-builder
Blackman, Edwin, clerk, H. H. Magie & Co.
Blanchard, Francis G., real estate dealer, Lake street
Blanchard, Joseph, carpenter and builder,
Blair, George, tailor, (Manierre & Blair) h 260 State st
Blakesley, Harvey A., bookkeeper, L. W. Holmes
Blasy, Barnhard, baker, Randolph st
Blatchford, Rev. John, Presbyterian Church, Clark street
Bliss, Charles, carpenter, State street
Blodgett, Caleb, brick maker, North Water street near N. Wells
Blodgett, Henry W., clerk, Philip F. W. Peck
Blodgett, Tyler K., tavern-keeper, Michigan ave
Boardman, Dr. Henry K. W., Clark street
Boggs, Charles F., carpenter, Webster & Boggs
Bolles, Nathan H., county commissioner, overseer poor, Lake st
Bolles, Peter, school inspector, Wells st near Randolph
Bond, Heman, horse dealer, Adams st near State
Bond, Harvey, stage-driver
Bond, James, painter,
Bond, William, laborer,
Boone, Levi D., physician, State street, cor. Washington st
Boes, John, house mover, cor. River and South Water street
Bosworth, Increase, Edwards & Bosworth
Borein, Rev. Peter R., pastor Methodist Church, Washington st
Botsford & Beers, copper, tin and sheetiron, cor. Lake & Dearborn
Botsford, Jabez K., Botsford & Beers
Botsford, Moss, clerk, Botsford & Beers
Bowen, Erastus, city collector, So. Water st, cor. Michigan ave.

Bowen, Henry, wagon maker, Wabash ave. near Randolph st
Boyce, L. M., wholesale druggist and apothecary, 121 Lake st
Boyer, Charles, clerk, on the canal
Boyer, John K., coroner, South Water street near Clark
Boyer, Dr. Valentine A., South Water st near Clark
Boyd, Robert, canal contractor, Boyd & Zell
Boyland, William, carpenter, VanBuren street, near LaSalle
Bracken, John, canal contractor, Canal street near Randolph
Brackett, Wm. W., city clerk, court house, Clark st
Bradley, Asa F., city surveyor, Morrison's Row, Clark street
Bradley, Cyrus P., check clerk, H. Norton & Co.'s warehouse
Bradley, David, plow maker, Asahel Pierce
Bradley, David M., foreman Chicago Democrat, 107 Lake st
Bradley, Timothy M., check clerk, Norton & Co.'s warehouse
Brady, George, constable, alley bet. North Water and Kinzie st
Brainard, Dr. Daniel, 17 Dearborn st
Brand, Alex., banker, (Murray & Brand)
Breese, Josiah S., Taylor, Breese & Co.
Breese, Robert, clerk, James Hervey
Bridges, Thomas B., carpenter, bds Philo Carpenter
Briggs & Humphrey, carriage and wagon makers, Randolph st
Briggs, Benjamin, wagon-maker, Briggs & Humphrey
Brinkerhoff, Dr. John, 49 Clark st
Bristol, Calvin, canal contractor
Bristol, Capt. Levi, schooner Jefferson
Bristol (Robt. C.) & Porter (Hibbard), agents for C. M. Reed,
    forward. commission merchants, cor. State and So. Water sts
Brock, John, clerk, John Parker
Brock, Mrs. Mary, millinery and straw bonnets, Lake street
Brock, Michael, carpenter, Lake street near Franklin
Brock, Thomas, ex-justice of peace, cor. Madison and Clark
Brookes, Henry, clerk, bds. Samuel Brookes
Brookes, Joshua, clerk, Stephen F. Gale
Brookes, Samuel, florist, Adams street near Dearborn
Brookes, Samuel M., portrait painter, Adams street
Brooks, Charles, clerk, B. T. Hunt
Brooks, Capt. ——, schooner Jessie Smith
Brooks, James, carpenter, Peter Graff
Brooks, Thomas, tailor, (McCracken & Brooks)
Brooks, William, carpenter and joiner
Brown, Andrew J., student, Henry Brown
Brown, George, chair maker, Lake street, near Franklin
Brown, Henry, attorney and counsellor at law, Clark st
Brown, John, porter, Illinois Exchange
Brown, Joseph E., carpenter and builder, Clark st near Jackson
Brown, Lemuel, blacksmith, Randolph street near Dearborn
Brown, Nathaniel J., canal contractor
Brown, Rufus B., warehouseman, Bristol & Porter
Brown, William H., cashier, Branch State Bank Illinois, La-
    Salle st cor. So. Water
Brown, Charles E., clerk, Horatio O. Stone
Bruce, Duncan,
Buchannan, Nelson, druggist, W. H. & A. F. Clarke

CHICAGO DIRECTORY. 9

Buck, Henry, boarding-house, Michigan ave. near Washington st
Burbeck, Isaac, butcher, Hovey & Burbeck
Burgess, John, wagon maker, Randolph st, east of Wells
Burke, Charles, actor, Chicago Theatre,
Burke, M., tender South Branch bridge
Burkett, Thomas, drayman
Burley, Arthur G., crockery, stone, and earthenware, 161 Lake
Burley, Augustus H., clerk, Stephen F. Gale
Burley, Charles, clerk, Stephen F. Gale
Burnum, Ambrose, canal contractor
Burnett, John, drayman, Illinois st. east of Pine
Burton, John, gardener, North Dearborn st, near North ave
Burton, Horace, clerk,
Burton, Stiles, grocer and liquor dealer, cor. Lake and State sts
Busch, John B., blacksmith and horseshoer, 16 Clark st
Bush, William, clerk, Charles Walker & Co.
Butler, John H., carpenter, 154 Clark street
Butler, Nathaniel, tinner,
Butterfield, Justin, attorney and counsellor at law, 46 Dearborn st
    res. Michigan st. cor. Rush
Butterfield, jr., Justin, law student, Butterfield & Collins
Butterfield, George, bds Justin Butterfield
Butterfield, Lyman, Columbian House, Wells st cor. S. Water
Butterfield, William, medical student, bds Justin Butterfield
Butterfield, J. Carver, compositor, Daily American office
Buzzard, Solomon, wood merchant, West Kinzie street
Byrnes, Michael, hostler, Tremont House

Caldwell, Billy, North Branch Chicago river, 5th ward
Cadwell, Caleb, teamster, North side
Cadwell, Philemus, teamster, North side
Calhoun, Alvin, carpenter and builder, 58 Randolph st
Calhoun, John, county collector, Eddy's store, 105 Lake st
Campbell, George, Goodsell & Campbell
Campbell, George L., clerk, Capt. John B. F. Russell
Campbell, James, carpenter and builder, State st
Campbell, James, compositor, Daily American office
Campbell, John, whitewasher and laborer, Ohio st. near LaSalle
Campbell, Major James B., real estate agent, North Clark street
Canda, Florimond, farmer, North Wells street
Carli, Paul, candies and notions, South Water st. near Wells
Carlin, Philip, blacksmith, Frink & Walker
Carling, John, clerk, James Killick
Carling, William, carpenter, bds. J. Outhet
Carney, James, grocery and provision store, 133 Lake st
Carney, Patrick, laborer, Carney's boarding-house
Carpenter, Job, gardener, 554 West Lake st
Carpenter, Joseph, milkman, 570 West Lake st
Carpenter, Philo, druggist and apothecary, South Water st
Carpenter, Samuel, ferryman at Clark street
Carpenter, William, grocer, 578 West Lake st
Carr, William and Samuel, bakers, North Water street
Carroll, Edward, drayman, Michigan street

Carter & Co., Thomas B., fancy dry goods, etc., 118 Lake st
Carver, Capt. David
Case, Capt. Calvin, shipbuilder, bds. Henry Wolcott
Casey, Edward, clerk, Stanton & Black
Casey, John, bricklayer, cor. Market and Washington streets
Casey, Patrick, waiter, Mansion House
Casey, Peter, clerk, Stanton & Black
Casey, Stephen, driver, Eli S. Prescott
Cassaday, Patrick E., surveyor, bds. Green Tree
Caswell, Sidney, cabinet maker, John B. Weir
Caton, John D., attorney at law, Clark street
Cauker, Mat., Steamboat Hotel, North Water st. near Kinzie
Cavanaugh, Martin, laborer, North Water street near Franklin
Chacksfield, George, grocery and provision store, South Water
    near Clark st
Chamberlaine, J. S., attorney, (Hamilton & Chamberlaine)
Chandler, Joseph, harbor Government works
Chapin, John P., commission merchant, South Water st
Chapin, Orlando, boarding-house, Clark street
Chapman, Charles H., real estate dealer, Randolph street
Chapman, George H., real estate dealer
Chapman, William W., clerk,
Chapron, A., laborer, North Water street near Market
Chapron, Francis, gardener, West Water street, north end
Charleston, Charles, carpenter, North State street
Childs, Shubael D., engraver, Saloon Buildings, Clark street
Choulet, Michael, carpenter, Alex. Loyd
Christy, Nathan, fisherman, North Canal street near W. Lake
Church, Edward, clerk, Charles Walker & Co.
Church, Thomas, grocery and provision store, 111 Lake st
Church & Sheldon, dry goods and groceries, 158 Lake street
Church, William L., (Church & Sheldon)
Churchill, Jesse, herdsman,
Clarke, Abram F., druggist, W. H. & A. F. Clarke
Clark, Francis, clerk, Geo. W. Merrell
Clarke, Dr. Henry, 159 Lake street
Clarke, George P., druggist, Wm. H. & Abram F. Clarke
Clarke, George W., surveyor, on the canal
Clarke, Henry B., Michigan ave., cor. 16th street
Clarke, Henry W., attorney at law, 9 Clark street
Clark, John, (Hobbie & Clark)
Clark, Lewis W., lottery and exchange broker, 150½ Lake st
Clarke, Norman, dealer in land claims, etc.
Clarke, Samuel C., druggist
Clark, Thomas A., dry goods, Lake street near Clark
Clarke, Wm. H. & Abram F., wholesale druggists and apothe-
    caries, 128 Lake street cor. Clark
Claus, Joseph, harbor Government works
Claus & Teetard, cabinet makers, 20 LaSalle st.
Cleveland & Co., house, sign, ornamental painters, Dearborn st
Cleaver, Charles, candle and soap factory, on South Branch
Cleaver, Thomas B., soapmaker, Charles Cleaver
Clifford, Thomas, carpenter, Lake street bet Clark and LaSalle

Clybourn, Archibald, farmer and cattle-dealer, 512 Elston ave
Cobb, Silas B., saddle, harness, and trunk maker, 171 Lake st
Coffin, J. W. C., dry goods, etc., South Water st. near LaSalle
Cogshall, Rev. Selah W., school-teacher, Market street
Cohen, Peter, merchant, South Water street
Cole, A., ship, house, sign, and ornamental painter, 129 Lake st
Cole, Parker M., dry goods and groceries, Lake street
Coleman, Ira, foreman, Daniel Taylor
Collins, George, (S. B. Collins & Co.)
Collins, George C., school-teacher, Lake street
Collins, Isaac, boot and shoe dealer, S. B. Collins & Co.
Collins, Jas. H., attorney and counsellor at law, 46 Dearborn st
Collins, John, boot and shoemaker, Canal street near VanBuren
Collins, John, 6th ward
Collins, Samuel B. & Co., boots, shoes, and leather, 140 Lake
Colvin, Edwin B., doors and sash, cor. N. Water & N. Dearborn
Conklin, J., blacksmith, carriage and wagon repairer, 47 Clark st
Conley, John, teamster, North Water st near LaSalle
Connell, J., laborer, Dearborn street bridge
Constantine, Pat., laborer, Illinois street near North LaSalle
Cook, Alfred, speculator, bds Illinois Exchange
Cook, C. W., Illinois Exchange, 192-6 Lake st, cor. Wells st
Cook, George C., clerk, Thomas Church
Cooke, Horatio N., turner, Franklin st
Cook, Isaac, Eagle saloon, 10 Dearborn st
Cook, John, baker, LaSalle street
Cook, John, tailor, John H. Hodgson
Cook, Thomas, teamster, Desplaines st near Monroe
Cooper, ——, teamster,
Copp, Thomas, tailor, Lake street
Corrigan, William, drayman, South Water st
Couch, Ira, hotel-keeper, Tremont House, n.-w. cor. Dearborn
  and Lake sts
Couch, Ira H., bds. Tremont House
Couch, James, Superintendent Tremont House
Countryman, ——, farmer, West Randolph street
Cox, A. Jackson, tailor, 9 Clark st
Cox, David, hotel-keeper, cor. West Lake and North Canal sts
Cox, John, drayman, North Water street
Cram, Capt. T. J., U. S. topographical engineer, Garrison
Crane, Capt. Leander,
Crawford, George, canal contractor, Crawford & Hervey
Crawford & Hervey, dry goods and groceries, North Water st
Crawford, William, drayman, alley bt North Clark and LaSalle
Crocker, Hans, attorney at law,
Crosman, Perry L., Crosman & Mathes
Crosman & Mathes, commission, groceries, liquors, 156 Lake st
Cruver, John, carpenter, Cruver & Sensor
Culver, Charles, cooper, cor. North Union st and Milwaukee av
Cunningham, Henry, grocery, North Water st. cor. N. Dearborn
Cure, John, helper, Briggs & Humphrey
Cure, Peter, grocery and provision store, Randolph st
Curtiss, Eli, clerk,
Curtiss, James, attorney and counsellor at law, 175 Lake st

Cushmar & Morris, sign painters

Daly, Barry, drayman
Daly, John, carpenter, North Water street near Dearborn
Daly, Thomas, drayman, North side
Daniels, Horace, carriage-driver, Graves' livery stable
Darrow, Sidney L., milkman, Lake shore, south side
David, Wm., boot and shoe maker, 176 Lake street
Davidson, Lars, fireman, steamboat Geo. W. Dole
Davidson, Peter, hostler, John H. Kinzie
Davidson, Sivert, carpenter, Cass street, Dutch Settlement
Davis, Miss A., cloak maker and tailoress, 115 Lake st
Davis, D. M. P., horse-dealer, 159 Michigan ave
Davis, Elisha W., clerk, Stiles Burton
Davis, George, county clerk, 109 Lake st
Davis, Horace, grocer and provisions, South Water street
Davis, John, tailor, North Water street, near Kinzie
Davis, Samuel N., lime burner, State st, near Adams
Davis, Wm. H., deputy-sheriff and constable, So. Water st
Davis, Kinzie & Hyde, hardware, Kinzie street near Cass
Davlin, Edward, farmer and teamster
Davlin, John, auctioneer, s.-w. cor. Dearborn and So. Water sts
Day, William, boarding-house, LaSalle street near Lake st
Dean, Philip, teamster, Madison street, near Franklin
Dellicker, George L., grocer and provision store, 163 Lake st
Dempsey, John, boarding-house, North Water st. near Clark
Dennis, Samuel C., dry goods, Lake street near Clark
Densmore. Eleazer W., clerk, R. P. & J. H. Woodworth.
Detrich, Veit, match maker, cor. Division and North State sts
Dewey, Dennis S., chair and furniture maker, 139 Lake street
Dewey, Dr. E., druggist and apothecary, 22 Dearborn st
DeWolf, Calvin, law student, Spring & Goodrich
Dexter, Albert A., clerk, R. P. & J. H. Woodworth
Diamond, Martin, laborer, North Water street
Dickey, Hugh, T., attorney and counsellor at law, 8 Clark st
Dickey, James V., fanning mill factory, North Clinton st
Dickinson, Augustus, porter, City Hotel
Dimmick, Edward, painter, (Wayman & Dimmick)
Dinjon, John, saloon and boarding-house, Franklin street
Dinmore, William, Dunn street
Diversy, Michael, milkman, Wm. Lill's brewery
Dixon, William, shipcarpenter, cor. N. Water and N. Dearborn
Dodge, Miss, school-teacher, Wells street
Dodge, Dupley, tailor, Clark street
Dodge & Tucker, ship chandlers and grocers, 147 South Water
Dodge, John C., Dodge & Tucker
Dodge, Lewis, carpenter
Dodge, Martin, salesman, lumber-yard, cor. N. Wells & Water
Dodge, Usual, carpenter,
Dodge & Austin, Drs., Lake street, west of Dearborn
Dodson, Christian B., contractor, West Lake street near Canal
Dodson, William S., contractor, West Lake street near Canal
Dole, George W., city treasurer, Michigan st
Dole, Lucius G., eye doctor,

Dolesey, Peter, saloon, Lake street
Dolton, George, tailor, North Water street
Doolittle, —, commission merchant, cor. Dearborn and S. Water
Donavan & Zell, auctioneers, South Water street
Doney, Jacob, cabinet maker, Michigan street near N. State
Donlin, John, grocery, North Clark street near N. Water
Donnelley, James M., carriage-driver, Graves' livery stable
Doty, Theodorus, deputy-sheriff, Randolph street near Clark
Dougall, Capt. Wm., schooner Drift
Downing, Thomas, butcher, Funk's market
Downs, Augustus G., clerk, Charles Walker & Co.
·Doyle, Elias,
Doyle, James H., meat market, 95 Lake street, Funk & Doyle
Doyle, Michael, Andrus & Doyle
Doyle, Simon, tailor, junction of Kinzie and North Water sts
Doyle, Simon, cattle drover
Drury, Benjamin, miller, Gage's mill
Duck, Dr. Charles H.
Duffey, Pat., saloon, North Water street
Duffy, James, plasterer, and assessor, 5th ward
Duncan, Thomas, tailor, Clark street
Dunham, David, carpenter, North Water street cor. N. Clark
Dunlap, M. L., grocer, North Water street
Dunlap, William, clerk, lumber-yard
Dunlop, Hugh, carpenter and builder, Illinois st
Durand, Chas., attorney and counsellor at law, 149 Lake st
Durant, James T., (Guild & Durant)
Duryee, Charles H., mathematical school, Cass street nr. Illinois
Dwyer, Cornelius, laborer, North Water street
Dye, John, clerk, Lake street
Dyer (Chas. V.) & Boone (Levi D.), Drs., office, 49 State street
Dyer, Thomas, commission merchant, South Water st

Eachus, Virgil H., tailor, Clark st
Eddy & Co., Ira B., hardware, stove, etc., 105 Lake street
Eddy, Devotion C., (Ira B. Eddy & Co.)
Edgel, Stephen M., real estate dealer, bds D. B. Heartt
Edwards, Alfred, grocery and provision store, North Water st
Edwards, Alfred, Edwards & Bosworth
Edwards, Francis, carpenter and joiner, 177 Lake st
Edwards & Bosworth, general store, South Water street
Edson, Robert, blacksmith, North Wells st
Egan, Dr. William B., real estate dealer, bds. City Hotel
Eggleston, ———, grocer and provisions, cor. Lake and Wells
Eldridge, Dr. John W., Clark st cor. S. Water, Loomis' Building
Elliott, James,
Ellis, Joel, butcher, Funk's Fulton market, 95 Lake street
Ellis, Samuel, milkman, south of 22d street, red barn on prairie
Ellithorpe, Albert C., fanning-mill factory, Monroe nr Franklin
Ellithorpe, Timothy C., compositor, Chicago Democrat office
Elston, Daniel, brickmaker, Elston road
Elston, Daniel T., student, Daniel Elston
Ely, Thomas, clerk, bds. Shakespeare Hotel
Emerson, Benjamin, milkman, Chicago ave. near Lill's brewery

Falch, Leonard, soap and candle maker, cor. LaSalle & Michigan
Farley, Alfred M., groceries and liquors, cor. Clark & S. Water
Farrell, Thomas, mason's laborer, 257 State st
Farwell, George, tinner, Ira B. Eddy & Bro.
Faxon & Co., general merchants, South Water street
Fennerty, John, fancy dry goods store, South Water street
Fennerty, James, with John Fennerty
Fennerty, Peter, auctioneer, John Davlin
Fergus, Robert, printer, 51 Clark street
Ferguson, Andrew, drayman, Wells st
Ferguson, James, Goodsell & Campbell
Ferson, Reed, farmer
Fillmore, Philetus, machinist, Stow's foundry
Finnemore, Richard, sawyer, North State st near North Water
Fischer, Peter H., wood turner, Franklin street near Randolph
Fitzgibbons, John, horse dealer, South Water street
Fitzgibbons, Patrick, drayman, River street
Fitzpatrick, John, laborer, cor. Chicago avenue and Rush street
Fitzsimmons, Michael, teamster, Michigan ave. cor. Congress
Fitzsimmons, Patrick, teamster, North Clark st. nr. North ave.
Flagg, Carlton, harness maker, Silas B. Cobb
Fleming, William, tailor, North Water st cor. North Dearborn
Flood, Capt. James
Flood, Capt. Peter, schooner Huron
Foley, Thomas, boot and shoemaker, Thomas Melvin
Follansbee, Alanson, grocery and provision store, 18 Dearborn st
Follansbee, Chas., grocery and provision store, 24 Dearborn st
Foot, David P., blacksmith, So. Water st
Foot, John P., blacksmith, Randolph street, near State
Foot, Star, teamster, Clark st cor. Monroe
Foot,   , tinner, Botsford & Beers
Ford, Bartley, boot and shoe maker, North Water st
Ford, Martin M., tanner, Clark street, n.e. cor. Nadison
Ford, William, baker, West Randolph street near the River
Fordham, Jared, boarding-house, LaSalle st, near Lake st
Forsyth, William, merchant, West Water street
Foster, Edward, general contractor, bds. Jas. West
Foster (Geo. F.) & Robb (Geo. A.), grocers and ship chandlers,
   cor. North Dearborn and North Water sts
Foster, Dr. John H., Lake street
Fralich, Frederick, baker, John Pfund
Frank, William, carpenter, Cass street near White
Freeman, Robert, carpenter, Clark street cor. Monroe
Freeman, William, sexton, St. James' Church, Cass street
Freer, L. C. Paine, attorney at law, Clark st
French, Wm. Bailey, real estate, Clark street
Frink (John) & (C. K.) Bingham, stage office, 123 Lake street
Frink, jr., John, clerk, Frink & Walker
Frink, Harvey, clerk, Post Office
Fry, Philip, clerk, L. F. Lewis
Fuller, Andrew, clerk, Vibbard & Tripp
Fuller, Henry L., clerk, Recorder's office
Fullerton, Alex. N., lumber merchant, North Water st
Fullagher, George, clerk, George Chacksfield

Fullagher, Samuel, carpenter,
Fullagher, Thomas, clerk, Shakespeare Hotel
Funk & Doyle, butchers, Fulton and Illinois markets, 95 Lake
street, and N. Water street, cor. North State
Funk, Absalom, Funk & Doyle, butchers
Funk, John, butcher, Absalom Funk
Funk, William, clerk, William Logan
Fussey, John, sawyer, West Monroe street cor. Canal

Gable, Peter, laborer, cor. Cass and Pearsons streets
Gage, George, surveyor, bds. John Gage
Gage, John, flour store, South Water st.; mill South Branch
Gage, Jared, flour dealer, South Water, bet. Clark and Dearborn
Gage, Leonard, milkman, Canal street near VanBuren
Gale, Abraham, 99 Lake street
Gale, Stephen F., bookseller and stationer, 159 Lake st, corner
Gale, Mrs. A., New York millinery store, 99 Lake st
Gallagher, William, butcher, North Water st
Gargen, Henry, laborer, cor. Rush and Pearsons streets
Garrett, Augustus, auctioneer, real estate, bds. Sauganash Hotel
Gates, Philetus W., machinist, 42–48 Canal street
Gaugler, Maurice, cabinetmaker, cor. Rush and Pearsons sts
Gavin, Edward, carpenter, Cass street near Kinzie
Gavin, Isaac R., Sheriff, Randolph st, n.-w., cor. Public Square
Gay, Dr. S. B., Canal street near Randolph
Gee, , distiller, North Water street near Market
Gee, , laborer, North Water street near Market
Gelderhüüs, Ole, carpenter, North Water street
George, Thomas, tinner, S. J. Surdam
Germon, Greene C., actor, Chicago Theatre
Getzler, Anton, hats, caps, umbrellas, etc., 151 Lake st
Gibbons, Edward, laborer, bds Henry Cunningham
Gibson, John, boarding-house, Randolph street
Gibson, John G., merchant
Gilbert, Ashley, bookkeeper, Horace Norton & Co.
Gilbert, Samuel H., clerk, Hobbie & Clark
Gilbert, Sherod, drayman, Ohio st. bet North State and Dearb.
Gilberton, Francis, laborer,
Gilberton, Ralph, laborer,
Giles, William, laborer, West Lake street, Philo Carpenter
Gill, Edmund, "Shakspeare", cor. North Water and Rush sts.
Gillen, Jacob, tailor, Rush street near Division
Gillenger, William, carpenter,
Gillespie, Eugene, Kinzie & Gillespie
Gillespie, John J., cabinet maker,
Gillinger, Jeremiah, clerk, J. L. Hanson
Gillis, Alexander, carpenter, Clark street cor. VanBuren
Gilmour, William, laborer, North Water street
Gilson, Hiram L., livery stable, Kent & Gilson
Goldan, John, mason, North Water street near North LaSalle
Goodenow, Aaron M., dry goods merchant, 134 Lake street
Goodhue, Dr. Josiah C., Dearborn street north of Lake street
Goodrich, Grant, attorney and counsellor at law, 107 Lake st
Goodrich, Henry, farmer, Dearborn street near Washington

Goodrich, T. Watson, clerk, T. B. Carter & Co.
Goodsell & Campbell, dry goods and grocery store, 21 Dearborn
Goodsell, L. B., Goodsell & Campbell
Goold, Nathaniel, grocery and provision store, 155 Lake st
Goss, Samuel W. & Co., dry goods merchants, 105 Lake st
Goss, John, Samuel W. Goss & Co.
Graff, Peter, carpenter, Franklin street bet Lake and Randolph
Granger, Elihu, iron foundry, North Water st, near LaSalle
Granger, Irving, foundryman, Elihu Granger
Grangien, Marks, laborer,
Grannis, Amos, carpenter, State street, cor. VanBuren
Grannis, Charles D., tinsmith, Botsford & Beers
Grannis, Samuel W., hatter, 16 Dearborn st
Grannis, Samuel J., shoemaker, South Water st
Grant, Jas., attorney, N. Water st near Rush, bds. Lake House
Graves, Dexter, livery stable, 44 State st, (Couch Place)
Graves, (D.) & Stevens, (M. W.), Rialto Saloon, 8 Dearborn st
Graves, Henry, State street near Lake st
Graves, Lorin, State street near Lake st
Graves, Sheldon, dealer in wooden-ware, Norton & Co.'s store
Graves, (Dot), Stephen R., merchant tailor, Clark street
Gray, Charles M., grain cradle factory, 78 Dearborn street
Gray, Franklin D., clerk, H. Norton & Co.
Gray, George M., agent, Charles M. Gray's factory
Gray, John, Chicago Hotel, cor. West Lake and North Canal sts
Gray, James, teamster, bds John Gray
Gray, John L., grocer, North Water st cor. Clark
Gray, Joseph H., dry goods and groceries, Lake street
Gray, William B. H., clerk, Joseph H. Gray
Green, C. L., actor, Chicago Theatre
Green, Russell, clerk, J. M. Underwood
Green, George W., farmer, Hardscrabble, 12th st. near Throop
Green, Walter R., hotel-clerk, Mansion House
Greenwood, John, teamster, Wm. Lill's brewery
Greenwood, Gay, clerk, Buckner S. Morris
Greenwood, Samuel, canal contractor, Illinois street near Cass
Greenwood, Theophilus, bookkeeper, G. S. Hubbard & Co.
Gregg, David R., carpenter, North Water street, near Kinzie
Gregory, Edward M., grocer, 9 Dearborn street
Greer, Samuel, carpenter and builder, N. Water near Franklin
Groll, Philip, baker, 51 LaSalle street
Groves, Alexander M. C. K., canal contractor
Guild & Durant, dry goods, etc., 149 Lake street
Guild, Albert H., (Guild & Durant)
Gunter, John, sailor, cor. Cass and Indiana streets
Gurnee, Walter S., Gurnee & Matteson
Gurnee & Matteson, wholesale saddlery hardware, 106 Lake st

Haas, William, brewer, cor. Chicago avenue and Pine street
Haddock, Edward H., commission merchant, South Water st
Haffey, Michael, carpenter, cor. North Water and N. Clark sts
Hageman, James, tinsmith, Botsford & Beers
Hahn, Adam, teamster,
Haight, Isaac, North Canal street near West Lake

Haight, Mrs. E., boarding-house, Clark street near Washington
Haines, Elijah M., tailor, S. Water st. bet. Clark and LaSalle
Haines, John C., clerk, George W. Merrill
Hale, Benjamin F., botanic physician
Hall, Henry P., barber, Rush street, on the River, nr N. Water
Hall, Philip A., clerk,
Hall, J. B., steamboat runner
Hallam, Edward S., Stearns & Hallam
Hallam, Rev. Isaac W., St. James' church, Cass st. nr. Illinois
Hamilton, Amos C., clerk, B. F. Knapp
Hamilton, Polemus D., carpenter, Clark street
Hamilton, Rich'd J., clerk circuit court, Clark st cor. Randolph
Hamilton, Robert P., groceries and provisions, Lake st
Hamilton, Thomas E., carpenter, Madison street cor. LaSalle
Hanchett, John L., surveyor and engineer, on the Canal
Handy, Joy, bricklayer and plasterer
Handy, Major, bricklayer and plasterer,
Hanlon, Edward, blacksmith, on the canal
Hanlon, Michael, blacksmith and horse-shoer, Ohio street
Hanson, Joseph L., grocery and provision store, 146 Lake st
Harban, Matthias, shoemaker,
Harding, Capt. Charles, schooner Gen. Thornton, bds. Tremont
Harding, Francis, attorney at law, Lake street
Harkness, Larned B., real estate operator
Harman, Wm., blacksmith, North Water st, near North State
Harmon, Dr. Elijah D.
Harmon, Isaac D., dry goods merchant, 8 Clark street
Harmon, (Chas. L.) Loomis (Horatio G.) & Co., wholesale gro-
cers, s.-w. cor. Clark and So. Water sts
Harmon, Edwin R., clerk, Harmon & Loomis
Harmon, J., grocery store, South Water st, near State
Harper, Richard, (called "Old Harper," vag.)
Harrington, Rev. Jos., First Unitarian Church, bds Lake House
Harris, Jacob, carpenter and builder, Adams street
Harris, John, gardener, n.-w. cor. Washington and Desplaines
Harrison, John, carpenter,
Harrison, H. H., harness maker, S. B. Cobb
Harrison, Thomas, drayman, Luther Nichols
Harvey, Edward, saloon and boarding-house, Kinzie near Rush
Hastings, Heman, farmer, Clark street cor. Adams
Hastings, Hiram, cattle dealer, 211 Clark street cor. Adams
Hatch, David, cutlery, hardware, etc., 98 Lake st
Hatch, Heman, saloon keeper, Dearborn street
Hatch, John, driver, Robert A. Kinzie
Hatch, ——, West India goods, South Water street
Hatfield, Isaac P., bookkeeper, Daily American office
Haven, Dr. Simon Z., Lake street, west of Tremont House
Hawkins, John, sailor
Hawkins, Capt. Henry
Hawley, John C., clerk, H. H. Magie & Co.
Hayden, James, drayman, 84 Wabash avenue
Hayes, Joel N., clerk, William B. Ogden
Haywood & Co., burr mill stone manufactory, Kinzie st
Heacock, Reuben B., medical student, Dr. C. V. Dyer

Heacock, Russell E., att'y, justice of peace, Adams cor. Clark
Heacock, jr., R. E., civil engineer, on the canal,
Heacock, Walstien, horse-rider, bds. R. E. Heacock
Heacock, William O., student, bds. R. E. Heacock
Heald, Alexander H., mason builder, Jefferson st
Heald, jr., Daniel, plasterer, Jackson st west of Clark
Healey, Robert, farmer, Archer Road near Halsted street
Heartt, Chauncy B., clerk, bds Daniel B. Heartt
Heartt, Daniel B., constable, Wells st. cor. alley so. of Randolph
Heartt, Robert, driver, Kinzie & Hunter
Helm, Edwin, clerk, Kinzie & Hunter
Henry, Hugh K., carpenter, North Water street
Henson, Oliver C., hair-cutting and shaving shop, 183 Lake st
Herrick, Elijah W., canal contractor, bds. Tremont House
Herrick, Ira N., canal contractor, bds Tremont House
Hervey, James, canal contractor, Crawford & H., Indiana street
Hervey, James, (Sir), Crawford & Hervey
Hessey, William, ready-made clothing, Randolph st near bridge
Hettich, Louis, boarding and saloon, Clark st. nr. South Water
Heymann, F. T., watchmaker and jeweller, 173 Lake st
Hickey, Patrick, drayman, bds Chas. McDonnell
Higgins, A. D., dry goods, groceries, hardware, 132 Lake st
Higgins, Edward, cowfeeder, Tyler st
Higgins, Floyd, milkman, Tyler st
Higgins, Pat., laborer, bds Henry Cunningham
Higgins, W. B, dry goods, groceries, etc., 136 Lake street
High, jr., John, (H. H. Magie & Co.)
Hill, Auronah, carpenter, bds. John Gage
Hill, James, provision store, West Randolph street
Hill, Lansing, lime burner, Reed Lewis
Hills, William H., clerk, Horace Norton & Co.
Hilliard, Lorin P., bookkeeper, Charles Walker & Co.
Hines, Austin, tailor, North Water street
Hinton, Rev. Isaac Taylor, First Baptist Church, LaSalle st
Hitchkiss, Orin, tinner, Wm. Wheeler & Co.
Hobbie (Albert G.) & Clark (John), dry goods, etc., 142 Lake st
Hodgson, John H., tailor and clothier, 61 Clark street
Hoffmann, Francis A., bookbinder, Hugh Ross
Hogan, John S. C., dry goods and groceries, 236 Lake street
Hogan, Charles P., dry goods and groceries, Lake near Franklin
Hoag, Charles, bookkeeper, Newberry & Dole
Holbrook, John, boots and shoes, South Water street
Holcomb, Charles N., foreman, Daily American office
Holden, Charles N., (Parsons & Holden)
Holland, Charles, clerk, Liberty Bigelow
Holmes, Isaac, carpenter, Wells street
Holmes, Isaac, machinist, Stow's foundry
Holmes, Joseph and Wm., bartenders, Heman Hatch
Holmes, L. W., hardware and stove merchant, South Water st
Holmes, William, printer, Chicago Democrat office
Holsman, George, saloon, Lake street near LaSalle
Holt, John R., cashier, James A. Marshall
Hood, David, butcher, cor. North State and N. Water streets
Hooker, John W., grocery and provision store, 152 Lake street

Hooker, James L., clerk, Joseph H. Gray
Hopple, John J., clerk, James A. Smith & Co.
Horan, Owen, boarding-house and saloon, south on Clark street
Horton, Barney, saloon and ball-alley, South Water st
Horton, Dennison, harness maker, Lake st
Horner, John, plasterer, mason, etc., Ontario st, near the lake
Hosmer, Charles B., attorney at law,
Hossack, William, confectioner, 147 Lake street
Howe, Francis, baker, James L. Howe
Hough, Oramel S., with Sylvester Marsh
Hough, R. M., with Sylvester Marsh
Hough, Thomas, laborer, Wm. Hough
Hough, Wm., plasterer and bricklayer, LaSalle cor. Chicago av
Houghton, D. F., hotel-keeper, Sauganash Hotel
Hovey & Burbeck, butchers, Lake Street Market, 143 Lake st
Hovey, Samuel S., butcher, Hovey & Burbeck
Howard, A. H., deputy-sheriff
Howard, John M., druggist, W. H. & A. F. Clarke
Howe, Frederick A., justice of the peace, 97 Lake st
Howe, Frank, clerk, Branch State Bank of Illinois
Howe, James L., city bakehouse, Kinzie st, near Rush
Howe, Miss, milliner and mantua-maker, cor. Lake and Wells sts
Hoyne, Thomas, attorney and counsellor at law, 107 Lake st
Hubbard, Elijah K., banker, 47-51 Dearborn st
Hubbard & Co., Gurdon S., forwarding, and commission merchants, North Water st near Rush
Hubbard, Henry G., at G. S. Hubbard & Co.'s warehouse
Hubbard, Moses, clerk, Eli B. Williams, South Water st
Hubbard, Thomas R., attorney at law, Clark street, cor. Lake
Hughes, James, drayman, 294 Illinois street
Hugunin, Daniel, ship chandler, Hugunin & Pierce
Hugunin, Hiram, merchant, West Water street near Lake st
Hugunin, James R., clerk, L. W. Holmes
Hugunin, John C., dry goods and groceries, West Water street
Hugunin, Leonard C., speculator
Hugunin, Capt. Robert,
Hugunin & Pierce, ship chandlers, North Water cor. Dearborn
Hulbert, Eri B., (Chas. Walker & Co.)
Humphrey, James O., wagon-maker, (Briggs & Humphrey)
Hunt, Bela T., feather beds, mattresses, South Water street
Hunter, Capt. David, Illinois street, near Rush
Hunter, Edward H., deputy-sheriff, ex-justice of peace, Wells st
Huntington, Alonzo, attorney and counsellor at law, Lake st
Huntoon, Capt. Bemsley, steam saw mill, North Branch
Huntoon, Geo. M., constable, North State street near Kinzie
Hupp, S., ladies and gents' tailor and cutter, 210 Lake street
Hyde, Thomas, Davis, Kinzie & Hyde

Iliff, R. W., dry goods merchant, Ayres & Iliff
Illingworth, James O., bookkeeper, Crawford & Hervey
Ingersoll, Mrs., actress and teacher of dancing, bds Lake House

Jackson, Carding, farmer, Vincennes ave
Jackson, Cyrus, farmer, Vincennes ave
Jackson, Ezra, bds Samuel Jackson

Jackson, John, butcher,
Jackson, Richard, Southern Hotel, State street cor. Twelfth
Jackson, Samuel T., Government works, near Garrison
Jackson, Wm. W., clerk, H. W. Bigelow
Jackson, Capt. ———, sailor
James, 'Thomas, machinist, Stow's foundry
Jamieson, Capt. Louis T., Garrison
Jefferson & McKenzie, managers Chicago Theatre, Dearborn st
Jefferson, Joseph, Jefferson & McKenzie
Jefferson, Joseph, (Joe,) comedian, Chicago Theatre
Jefferson, Thomas, actor, Chicago Theatre
Jeffries, George, laborer, Rush street bet. Michigan and Illinois
Jenkins, Thomas, dry goods, etc., Lake street near Clark
Johnston, Adam, school-teacher, Dearborn street
Johnson, Andrew B., waiter, John H. Kinzie
Johnson, Anfen, with Simon Doyle, tailor, Kinzie street
Johnston, Anthony, steward, Lake House
Johnson, Baar, laborer, Cass street, Dutch Settlement
Johnston, Benj. W., carpenter
Johnston, James, drayman, Wabash ave. near Adams street
Johnson John, blacksmith, Joseph Willemin
Johnston, John, carpenter,
Johnson, John, haircutting and shaving-shop, 131 Lake st
Johnson, John, laborer, Cass street, Dutch Settlement
Johnston, Joseph, soap manufacturer, West Washington street
Johnson, J., dry goods aud groceries, Lake street
Johnston, Lathrop, bds New York House
Johnston, Samuel, bds New York House
Johnston, Sanford, carpenter, bds Chicago Hotel
Johnston, Capt. Seth, North Branch, west side
Johnston, jr., Seth, student, Dr. Stuart
•Johnson, William, haircutting and shaving saloon, Clark street
Jolisaint, Jean Pierre, laborer, Joseph Willemin
Jones, Benjamin, grocer, South Water street
Jones, D. A., cabinet and chair maker, Dearborn street
Jones, Elisha M., cabinet and chair maker, Dearborn street
Jones, Fernando, clerk, Thomas Church
Jones, Hiram, bds. Randolph street cor. Dearborn
Jones, King & Co., wholesale hardware merchants, So. Water st
Jones, Nathaniel A., clerk, John W. Hooker
Jones, Wm., justice of the peace, Dearborn st, cor. Randolph
Joyce, Thomas, grocery, North Clark street
Judd, Norman B., attorney and counsellor at law, 105 Lake st

Kane, James, carpenter,
Kane, Patrick, drayman, Kinzie street near N. LaSalle
Kaphahn, Godfrey, laborer, cor. Cass and Chestnut streets
Kastler, Matthias, laborer,
Kastler, Nicholas, shoemaker,
Kautenburger, Nicholas, laborer,
Keefe, James, laborer, North LaSalle street near White
Keefe, Owen, gardener, Division street near North Wells
Keenan, John J., vapor baths, Lake street cor. Wells
Kehoe, Capt. James, bds City Refectory; Dearborn street

Kehoe, Michael, drayman, 257 South Jefferson street
Keith,   , carpenter, Alexander Loyd
Kelly, James, compositor, Daily American office, h 145 Clark
Kelly, Capt. Patrick, boarding-house, North Water street
Kelsey, Patrick, laborer, Chicago ave near North Dearborn st
Kendall, Elihu, Smead, Kendall & Co.
Kendall, Vail & Co., clothing store 119 Lake str
Kennedy, Michael, 5th ward
Kennicott, Dr. Wm. H., dentist, Lake street
Kent & Gilson, livery stable, State st. (Tremont House alley)
Kent, B. H., livery stables, Kent & Gilson
Kent, Rev. Trumble, (Methodist) Monroe street near State
Keogh, P. R., tailor and clothier, Clark st
Kerchival, Gholson, real estate, River street
Kerchival, Lewis C., inspector Port of Chicago, bds City Hotel
Ketchum, ————, clerk, Gurdon S. Hubbard & Co.
Killick, James, grocery and provision store, 12 Dearborn st
Kimball, Granville, stage contractor, Frink, Walker & Co.
Kimball, Harlow, merchant, Clark street
Kimball, Henry N., vessel owner,
Kimball, Mark, clerk, 155½ Lake street
Kimball, Martin N., farmer and hay dealer, Milwaukee ave
Kimball, Walter, probate judge, cor. Clark and South Water st
Kimberly, Dr. Edmund S., res. N. Water st next Lake House
King, Byram, Jones, King & Co.
King, jr., John, merchant, bds. Lake House
King, Joe, (pork an' a bean) restaurant, South Water near Clark
King, Joseph, drayman,
King, Henry, dry goods, etc., North Dearborn st. near Kinzie
King, Nathaniel, clerk, Tuthill King
King, Richard, farmer
King, Tuthill, New York clothing store, 115 Lake st
King, Willis, lumber merchant, Randolph st. bridge
Kingswell, Wm., millwright, Wabash ave near VanBuren st
Kinzie, James, real estate agent, North Canal street
Kinzie (John H.) & Hunter (David), forwarding, commission
    merchants, North Water st. near Rush
Kinzie, Robert A., Davis, Kinzie & Hyde, Kinzie street
Klear, Frank, musician, State street near Harmon court
Knapp, Benj. F., salt merchant, South Water street near Clark
Knickerbocker, Abraham V., clerk, Government Works
Knight, John, drayman, Michigan ave, near Adams
Knight, Joseph, porter, Gurdon S. Hubbard & Co.
Knights, Darius, carpenter, with Alexander Loyd
Knox, James H., tanner, Wells street, south of Polk
Laflin, George H., clerk, Mathew Laflin
Laflin, Matthew, gunpowder and canal contrac'r, Washington st
LaBot, François, dyer and scourer
LaFromboise, Claude
LaFromboise, Eugene, Indian chief, res. Canal street
LaFromboise, Joseph, Indian chief
Lamb, Horace, ship carpenter, Michigan ave. near Lake street
Lane, Elisha, clerk, Botsford & Beers
Lane, Geo. W., clerk, A. Follansbee

Lane, James, boarding-house, North Water street cor. Dearborn
Landon, George, carpenter, Chicago ave near Sedgwick street
Landon, Thomas, carpenter, Chicago ave near Townsend street
Lang, John, carriage maker, etc., North State street near Kinzie
Lansing, Cornelius, clerk, Osborn & Strail
Lanswerk, Ole, laborer, North Water street
Lantry, Michael, teamster, Kinzie st
LaPoint, Pierre, blacksmith, Joseph Willemin
Lappin, Richard, teamster, Chicago ave cor. North State
Larrabee, William M., bookkeeper, Wm. B. Ogden
Larson, Andrew, laborer, Cass street, Dutch Settlement
Larson, John, sailor
Lawrence, Asa, wood merchant, North Water street
Lawson, Andrew, wood-sawyer, cor. North State and Hinsdale
Lawson, Canute, city street carpenter, 240 Superior street
Lawson, Iver, laborer, bds. 240 Superior street
Leary, Albert G., attorney and counsellor at law, Dearborn st
Leavenworth, Jesse H., supt. U. S. works, Fort Dearborn
Lee, Benj. Tyler, clerk
Lee, David S., attorney at law, Lake street
Legg, George, contractor and street maker, Grand ave. 6th ward
Legg, Isaac, real estate dealer, 6th ward, near Lill's brewery
Legg, James, teamster and horse dealer, West side
Legg, Joseph, carpenter, west on river bank, south of Lake st
Legg, Mrs. Rachel, boarding-house, West Kinzie street
Letz, Frederick, locksmith
Letz, Jacob, boot and shoe maker, Thos. Whitlock
Lewis, A. B., Sunday school agent, LaSalle st
Lewis, L. F., grocer and dry goods, Dearborn st. near Lake
Lewis, Reed, lime burner, Archer road, Bridgeport
Licenring, Samuel, tailor, Clark street
Lill, Wm., brewer, Chicago ave. cor. Pine st
Lincoln,   , cabinet maker, Dennis S. Dewey
Lincoln, Solomon, tailor and clothier, 156 Lake st
Lind, Sylvester, carpenter, bds 55 Clark st.
Lindebner, J., tailor and cutter, Lake st
Livingston, John R., real estate agent, bds. Lake House
Lock, William, ready-made clothing, 101 Lake st
Logan, William, grocery, West Water street
Loomis, Horatio G., (Harmon & Loomis)
Long, Mrs. John, 21 North Wells st
Lothe, Sven, carpenter and builder, North Water street
Loupean, Antoine, gardener, West Water street, north end
Loux, Matthias, laborer,
Loux, Peter, blacksmith,
Lovecraft, A., draper and tailor, 9 Clark street
Lowe, James M., clerk, Circuit Court clerk's office
Lowe, Samuel J., high constable, deputy-sheriff, 125 Clark st
Lowe, Samuel A., student, J. Y. Scammon
Loyd, Alex., carpenter and builder, 51 Wells st
Lozier, Oliver, painter and glazier, cor. Canal and Jackson sts.
Ludwig, Charles, cooper, Simon Ludwig
Ludwig, Frederick, cooper, Simon Ludwig
Ludwig, Simon, cooper, cor. Pearsons and Cass streets

Ludwig, jr., Simon, cooper, Simon Ludwig
Lyman & Gage, millers, South Branch, Canal street
Lynch, Patrick, laborer,

McAuley, Patrick, laborer, bds Richard Lappin
McBride, Thomas, drayman, Clark street
McCabe, Patrick, porter, Tremont House
McCarthy, Owen, grocery, North Water st
McClure, Andrew, carpenter, (Updike & McClure)
McClure, Charles, carpenter,
McClure, Josiah E., McClure & Co.
McClure, Judge Samuel, lottery office Liberty Bigelow
McClure, N. Alex., bookkeeper, Seth T. Otis & Co.
McClure & Co., (strictly) commission merchants, 89 Lake street
McComber, Miss, milliner and dress maker, 165 Lake st
McConnell, Edward, gardener, Lumber st near Canal st
McConnell, John, bookkeeper, Seth T. Otis & Co.
McCord, Jason, Mosely & McCord
McCorrister, William, American Hotel, North Water street
McCracken, Oren, tailor, McCracken & Brooks
McCracken & Brooks, tailors and clothiers, 12 Clark street
McDaniel, Alexander, teamster, Michigan ave.
McDermott, Mrs. Anne S., milliner and dress maker, S. Water
McDonnell, Charles, grocery and provision store, 30 Market st
McDonnell, Dennis, sailor, North Dearborn street cor. Huron
McDonnell, Peter, laborer, bds Michael McDonnell
McDonnell, Michael, grocery, North Water street near N. State
McFall, Francis, sash, door, and blind factory, Market st
McGee, James, engineer, steamer Geo. W. Dole
McGee, William, engineer, steamer James Allen
McGlashan, Alexander, farmer,
McGlashan, John, gardener, Archer road, on river, near 25th st
McGovern, John, farmer, Madison street near Franklin
McGrath, ——, teamster,
McGraw, Edward, laborer, North Water st. near Dearborn
McGraw, James, farmer, West Madison st. near Western ave
McGraw, John, soap maker, North Water street near N. Clark
McGuire, Michael, laborer, North Water street near Dearborn
McHale, John, laborer, North Water street
McHenry, Hiram, mate, schooner Constitution
McHenry, Peter, (Black Pete,) cook, City Hotel
McIntosh, Capt. David, Ohio street bet. Pine and Sand sts
McIntosh, Capt. Wm., Franklin street bet. Randolph and Lake
McKay, Patrick, saloon, North Water st
McKay, Samuel, salesman, Eli B. Williams, North Water st
McKee, David, gunsmith, U.S., Garrison
McKenzie, Alexander, Theatre, Jefferson & McKenzie
McLean, Thomas, laborer, cor. Chicago avenue and Cass street
McLeod, Capt. Alexander, carpenter
McMahon, Patrick, tailor, North Water street near Dearborn
McMahon, Patrick, porter, Lake House
McNeil, Malcolm, ship carpenter, North Branch, nr Chicago av

Magie, Haines H., (H. H. Magie & Co.)

Magie & Co., H. H., dry goods merchants, 130 Lake st
Magill, Alexander W., clerk,
Magill, Arthur W.,
Magill, Julian, clerk, Kinzie & Hunter
Maher, Hugh, cooper, South Branch, south side
Mallory, Hiram, canal contractor
Mallory, Edward, clerk, Botsford & Beers
Malzacher, Louis, grocery and provision store, 181 Lake st
Manierre (Edward) & Blair (Geo.), merchant tailors, 43 Clark st
Manierre, George, attorney and counsellor at law, 105 Lake st
Mann, Cyrus, carpenter and builder, Clark street
Mann, Tielman, laborer,
Manning, Joel, secretary to Canal Commissioners
Marback, Joseph, veg't gardener, cor. Chicago ave and Rush st
Markle, Abram A., late Illinois Exchange, 192 Lake street
Markoe, Hartman, dry goods merchant, Lake street
Markus, Ole, turner, Cass street, Dutch Settlement
Marsh (Sylvester) & Dole (Geo. W.), butchers, Dearborn st
Marshall, James A., auctioneer, commission, etc., So. Water st
Mason, Louis, painter, bds Joseph Willemin
Massey, I. F., saddler and shoe dealer, 170 Lake st
Massey, Mrs., milliner and dress maker, 165 Lake st
Mathes, William J., Crosman & Mathes
Mathews, James, constable, 4th ward
Matteson, Joseph, Gurnee & Matteson
Matthews, Frederick, baker, James L. Howe
Matthews, George, blacksmith, Joseph Willemin
Matthews, P., dry goods merchant, 162 Lake st
Maxwell, Dr. Philip, Garrison
Maxwell, Thomas, laborer, 124 Illinois street
Meeker, Geo. W., attorney and counsellor at law, 150 Lake st
Meeker, Joseph, carpenter and builder, 165 Clark st
Mevelle, Peter, carpenter, Michigan ave. near Lake street
Melvin, Thomas, boot and shoe maker, South Water st
Merrick, Dr., 121 Lake st., house cor. Randolph and State st
Merrill, George W., dry goods merchant, 166 Lake st
Merrill, George, clerk, Geo. Chacksfield
Mess, George, contractor, Michigan ave. cor. South Water
Metz, Christopher, tinner, Wm. Wheeler & Co.
Miguly, Rudolph, grocer, Randolph street near LaSalle
Milleman, Andrew, laborer, North Clark street nr Fullerton av
Miller, Bernhart, shoemaker, Indiana street near North State
Miller, Daniel, shoemaker, Indiana street near North State
Miller, Capt. Harry, schooner St. Joseph
Miller, Jacob, blacksmith, North State street cor. Indiana
Miller, John, tanner, North Branch, fire warden, 4th ward
Miller, Robert, ship carpenter, near Garrison
Miller, William, clerk, Jas. M. Strode
Milliken, Isaac L., blacksmith, Wabash ave. near Randolph
Mills, John R., clerk, Mathew Laflin
Mills, M., grocery and provision store, 154 Lake st
Milne (Robert) & Morrison, (Alex.) lumber merchants, So. Water
    street near Franklin
Miltimore, Ira, steam sash and door factory, South Branch River

Mitchell, John B., boot and shoe maker, South Water st
Mitchell, Joseph, carpenter, Alex. Loyd
Mitchell, Mark, carpenter, Alex. Loyd
Mitchell, Wm., carpenter, Canal street cor. Madison
Mitchell, Mrs. Hannah Weed, private boarding, 112 LaSalle st
Mooney, Michael, blacksmith and horse shoer, Franklin st
Mooney, Peter, blacksmith and horse shoer, M. Mooney
Moore, David, school inspector, fire warden, 5th ward
Moore, David, miller, at the wind mill, above North ave
Moore, George, teamster, Clinton street near West Kinzie
Moore, Henry, attorney and counseller at law, 9 Clark st
Moore, Joseph, confectioner, South Water street near 5th ave
Moore, Reuben, real estate, Clark street
Moore, Robert, teamster, Clinton street near West Kinzie
Moore, Dr., West Randolph street
Montgomery, G. B. S., general merchant, 137 Lake st
Montgomery, L. W., United States Hotel
Montgomery, G. B. S., boot and shoe maker
Morgan, Caleb, cabinet maker, Bates & Morgan
Morgan, Patrick R., horse-rider, bds. "Rat's-castle," cor. West
    Water and North Canal sts
Morris, Buckner S., (alderman,) attorney, etc., Saloon Bdgs
Morris, Emanuel, ice cream, soda water, Cass street nr. Illinois
Morrison, Alexander, lumber dealer, Milne & Morrison
Morrison, Charles, drayman, 135 Clark street
Morrison, Daniel, drayman, 135 Clark street
Morrison, Eph., hat and cap factory, Dearborn st b Lake & S.W.
Morrison, Ephriam, jr., teamster, 111 Madison street
Morrison, Ezekiel, carpenter, 123 Clark st
Morrison, James M., carpenter, 131 Clark street
Morrison, John C., grocery and provision store, South Water st
Morrison, John H., grocery store, 190 Lake st
Morrison, Orsemus, street com., collector, coroner, 153 Clark st
Mosely (Flavel) & McCord (Jason), merchants, South Water st
Montjoy, William, tailor, John H. Hodgson
Mower, George W., clerk,
Mulford, Major E. H., Illinois street near State
Mulford, James H. & Edward H. jr., jewelers, etc., Dearborn st
Muller, Matthias, laborer, Rush street north of Chicago ave
Murphy, James K., clerk, John Fennerty
Murphy, John, United States Hotel, West Water cor. Randolph
Murphy, Edward, school-teacher
Murphy, Dr. Richard, 147 Lake street
Murphy & Titus, proprietors "Rat's-castle Hotel, W. Water st
    north of West Lake st
Murray, George, tailor and clothier, 198 Lake st
Murray (Jas.) & Brand (Alex.), exchange brokers, 189 Lake st
Murray, S. R., deputy-sheriff
Musham, William, porter, G. S. Hubbard & Co.
Myers, F., saloon, North Water street
Myrick, Willard F., hotel-keeper, Cottage Grove ave, between
    29th and 3th streets, near the race course.

Nelson, Andrew, with Dea. John Wright, cor. Madison street

Nelson, Andrew, laborer, cor. Cass and Chestnut streets
Nettleton, I., livery stable, Dearborn street, nr. South Water
Neudorf, Nicholas, laborer,
Newberry (Oliver) & Dole (Geo. W.), forwarding commission
    merchants, N. Water st cor. Rush
Newberry, Walter L., att'y and real est., office Newberry & Dole.
Newcome, J. C., sawyer, and grocery, North Water near Clark
Nichols, Luther, drayman, 50 Dearborn street
Nicholson, Edward, distiller, Illinois st. near the Lake
Nicholson, Capt. John, cor. Cass and White streets
Nicholson & Co., groceries and dry goods, North Water st
Nickols, Patterson, livery stable keeper, Kinzie st near N. State
Nightingale, Rev. Crawford, First Unitarian Society, Saloon
Noble, John, real estate, res. Dutchman's Point
Noble, Major, farmer, at now called Irving Park
Noble, sen., Mark, farmer, Dutchman's Point
Noble, Mark, real estate, res. Dutchman's Point
Northam, Robert R., clerk, J. W. Hooker
Norton, Henry, merchant, Wabash ave.
Norton, N.R., bridge-builder, n.-w. cor. N. State and Indiana sts
Norton, Theron, dry goods, (Paine & Norton) 117 Lake st
Norton & Co., Horace, grocers and provisions, South Water st

Oakes, Noyes, house mover, Clark street
Oatman, O., secretary, Chicago Hydraulic Company
Oberhart, Joseph, laborer,
Ogden, Wm. B., real estate dealer, Kinzie st near North State
Ogden, Mahlon D., attorney, Arnold & Ogden, Clark street
Oliver, John A., house, sign, and ornamental painter, Kinzie st
Onde, Peter, laborer, Cass street, Dutch Settlement
Orr, Brakey, carpenter and builder, Cass street near Huron
Osborn, Hon. Andrew D.
Osborn, William, boot, shoe, and leather merchant, 141 Lake st
Osbourn & Strail, hardware, stove, and iron merchants, 124 Lake
Osbourn, L. F., Osbourn & Strail
Osterhoudt, L. M., New York House, 180 Lake st.
Otis & Co., Seth T., hardware, iron, and stoves, 11, 13 Dearborn
Outhet, John C., wagon maker, 191 Randolph street
Outhet, John, boarding-house,
O'Brien, George, grocery and provision store, N. Water st
O'Brien, James, saloon, South Water street near Franklin
O'Conner, Jeremiah, blacksmith, North Water street
O'Connor, Martin, blacksmith, Randolph st
O'Malley, Charles, shoemaker, North Water street
O'Meara, Timothy, Rev., Catholic priest, cor. State and Lake
O'Neil, John, farmer, cor 22d and Halsted streets
O'Neil, Michael, carpenter, North Dearborn street near Kinzie

Packard, Robert, teamster, Randolph street
Page, Peter, mason builder, 150 Clark street
Page, Thomas, bank porter, Murray & Brand
Paine (Seth) & Norton (Theron), dry goods merchants, 117 Lake
Palmer, Isaac K., City wood inspector
Parish & Metcalf, general merchants, 132 Lake st

Parker, John, dry goods, groceries, and liquors, 134 Lake st
Parry, Samuel, carpenter
Parsons & Holden, grocery & provisions, cor. Lake and So. Water
Parsons, Edward, Parsons & Holden
Patrie, Philip, blacksmith,
Patterson, John G., steward, Illinois Exchange
Patterson, Orville, horse-dealer, bds. Cox's hotel
Payne, William,
Peacock (Jos.) & Thatcher, (David C.) gunsmiths, 153 Lake st
Peacock, Elijah, watchmaker and jeweller, 155 Lake street
Peacock, Joseph, gunsmith, Peacock & Thatcher
Pearsall, John, farmer, Holstein
Pearsall, Rolla, farmer, city limits, western
Pearson, Hon. John, judge Circuit Court of Cook County
Pearsons, Col. Hiram, real estate dealer, North Dearborn street
Pearsons, P. H., grocer and dry goods, cor. S. Water and Clark
Peaslee, Harvey L.,
Peaslee, Horace L., clerk, Harmon & Loomis
Peck, Azel, carpenter and builder, Clinton st
Peck, Burr, Wheeler & Peck
Peck, Charles E., harness maker, 164 Lake st
Peck, Ebenezer, att'y, and internal improvement Canal board
Peck, Philip F. W., real estate speculator, 242 Clark street
Penny, John, brickmaker, North Branch, 5th ward
Periolat, F. A., grocery and provision store, 126 Lake st
Periolat, Clemens, grocer, Lake street cor. Franklin
Perrior, William, musician, Chicago Theatre
Perry, Abijah S., barber, ex-justice of the peace, Reservation
Perry, Edward, and Brother, saloon, Clark street
Perry, Samuel, carpenter and joiner
Peters, George, clerk, Gurdon S. Hubbard & Co.
Peterson, Capt. George, Canal street
Pettet, John, Garrison
Peyton, Francis, attorney at law, Lake street
Peyton, Lucien, attorney at law, West Lake street nr. N. Canal
Pfund, John, bread and biscuit baker, 14 Clark st
Phelps, John, tinner, William Wheeler & Co.
Philips, Clifford S., wholesale dry goods merchant, 125 Lake st
Phillips, John F., tailor and clothier, City Hotel building, Clark
Pierce, Asahel, plow, and wagon maker, 18 Market street
Pierce, Smith D., ship chandler, North Water street
Pitkin, Nathaniel, dry goods, Sherman & Pitkin
Pitt, William, sawyer, North Canal st
Plummer, Enoch, plasterer, Adams st near State
Pond, William, watch and clock maker, 185 Lake st
Porter, Hibbard, (Bristol & Porter,)
Post, Dr. L., residence Lake House, office Dearborn street
Powell, George N., tavern-keeper, Milwaukee ave
Powers, William G., general merchant, bds Lake House
Praler, Adam, laborer,
Prescott, Eli S., receiver, United States Land Office, 175 Lake
Prescott, George W., clerk, James A. Marshall
Preston, John B., civil engineer
Price, Jeremiah, fire warden, South Water st near Wells

Price, Robert, tailor and clothier, 153 Lake st
Prindiville, John, steamer Dole
Prindiville, Maurice, contractor, n.w. cor. Chicago ave. N. State
Prindiville, Redmond, steamer Dole
Proctor, Dr., Dearborn st, north of Lake st
Pruyne, Peter, druggist and apothecary, South Water street

Rabbie, John Bat, bds LaFramboise
Raber, Philip, laborer, State street
Ragen, John G., cabinet-maker
Ralph, Peter, boot and shoemaker, Clark street near Randolph
Randolph, Geo. F., wholesale dry goods merchant; 109 Lake st
Rankin, David, boot and shoe maker, Illinois street nr Dearborn
Rankin, William & John, brassfounders, 55 Clark and Illinois st
Rathbone, Ward, groceries and provisions, 141 Lake st
Raynor, Jacob, grocery store, North Water street
Raymond & Co., Benj. W., general dry goods, etc., 122 Lake st
Raymond, George, clerk, B. W. Raymond
Reed, Chas. M., forwarding and commission merchant, South
    Water st cor. State
Reed, Frederick, porter, City Hotel, Clark street
Reed, Mrs., cloak and dressmaker, 115 Lake st
Reed, Thomas, teamster, 115 Lake street
Rees, James H., draughtsman and surveyor, Wm. B. Ogden
Reis, Jacob N., waterman, bds. 175 State street
Reis, John M., boot and shoe maker, Samuel J. Grannis
Reis, sen., John P., waterman, 175 State street
Reis, jun., John P., waterman, bds. 175 State street
Reis, Nicholas, waterman, 175 State st
Reis, Peter, waterman, 173 State st
Resique, Samuel, carpenter, Illinois street near Cass
Rew, Doc. Norman, saloon, South Water street near State
Reynolds, Eri, packer, Adams street
Rice, John, bartender, "Eagle" saloon, 10 Dearborn street
Richards, Alexander, clerk, David Hatch
Richards, Jas. J., clerk, Illinois street
Rider, E. A., clerk, C. L. P. Hogan
Riley, John, warehouseman, Newberry & Dole, Michigan st
Ripley, Capt. Calvin, steamer Geo. W. Dole
Rhines, Henry, deputy-sheriff and constable, 44 LaSalle st
Robb, George A., (Foster & Robb)
Roberts, David L., canal contractor
Roberts, George, carpenter, Alex. Loyd
Roberts, H. L., boot and shoe dealer, Lake street cor. LaSalle
Robertson, Cyrus D., clerk, H. H. Yates
Robertson, James, ship carpenter, North Water st. nr Dearborn
Robertson, Mrs., midwife, cor. North Water and N. Dearborn
Robinson, D. O., carpenter,
Robinson, James, carpenter, Clark street
Rockwell, James, furniture dealer, Lake street near Franklin
Roder, John, blacksmith, Joseph Willemin
Rogers, Edward K., (Horace Norton & Co.)
Rogers, George A., clerk, Horace Norton & Co.
Rogers, John, commission merchant, N. Water st. near N. State

Rogers, William, "the generous sport,"
Roi,   , laborer, North Water street near Market
Rooney, William, farmer, Maine
Ross, Hugh, bookbinder and paper ruler, 24 Clark st
Ross, Robert C., carpenter, North Dearborn st
Rossetter, Asher, Mansion House, 86 Lake st
Roth, John G., sausage maker, Absalom Funk
Rötter, Neils K., clerk, W. H. & A. F. Clarke
Rouscop, Jacob, teamster, cor. Rush and Whitney streets
Rowe, Jonathan,,sawyer, near Kinzie street bridge, 5th ward
Rowland, Treadwell, boarding-house, North State near Kinzie
Rucker, Henry L., alderman and justice of the peace, Dearborn
Rucker, Edward A., student, H. L. Rucker
Rudd, Edward H., job and book printer, Saloon Bdgs., Clark st
Ruddiman, John, moulder, Stow's foundry
Rue, John,,teamster, Ohio street
Rue, John C., carpenter and builder, 156 Clark st
Rumrill, B., watchmaker, James & Edward Mulford
Rumsey, George F., clerk, Newberry & Dole
Rumsey, Julian S., clerk, Newberry & Dole
Russ, John, farrier, Desplaines st, bet Jackson and VanBuren
Russell, Chester G., horse-dealer, Graves' livery stable
Russell, Francis, auctioneer, bds. Lake House
Russell, Jacob, City Hotel, Clark st, N.-W. cor. Randolph
Russell, Jacob, teamster, North side
Russell, Capt. John B. F., U.S.A., Indiana st. cor. North State
Russell, John J., teamster, North side
Russell, Dr. William., bds. City Hotel
Russell, William, teamster, North side
Russer, Frederick G., shoemaker, Rush street cor. Pearsons
Rutter, Capt. Solomon, bark Detroit
Ryan, Edward G., attorney and counsellor at law, 8 Clark st
Ryan, John, grocery and boarding-house, S. Water, nr River st

Sabine & Co., forwarding and commission merch'ts, Nor. Water
Sabine, William A., boarding-house, 161 Lake street, up stairs
Sabins, Carlos, tavern-keeper, Lake street
Sadler, Nicholas, gardener, Illinois street near North State
Saltonstall, William, fish dealer, West Madison street
Saltonstall, Wm W., bookkeeper, Hubbard & Co.'s warehouse
Sammons, Benjamin, cooper, Frederick Sammons
Sammons, E. W., cooper, Adams street
Sammons, Frederick, cooper, Clinton st
Sammons, Joel, cooper, Frederick Sammons
Sanger, James Y., canal contractor
Sanger, Lorenzo P., canal contractor
Satterlee, M. L., clerk, Thomas Church
Saunders, Robert Paul, grocer, South Water st, near State
Sauter, Chas. & Jacob, boot and shoemakers, 212 Lake st
Savage, Maurice, canal subcontractor, Michigan street nr Rush
Sawyer, Sidney, druggist and apothecary, 14 Dearborn st
Sawyer, Nathaniel, clerk, S. Sawyer
Scammon J. Young, attorney and counsellor at law, 105 Lake st
Schall, Andre, boarding-house and saloon, 191 Randolph st

Schaller, Andrew, provision and grocery store, 200 Lake street
Schenk, Henry, laborer, Chestnut street bet. Rush and Cass
Schmidt, Matthias, carpenter,
Schuttler, Peter, wagon maker, Randolph street near Franklin
Scougale, A., wagon maker, State street near Lake st
Scott, John, carpenter, South Branch, west side
Scott, William D., banker, Strachan & Scott
Scoville, Hiram H., machinist, 42-48 Canal street
Scoville, Ives, machinist
Scoville, James A., clerk, Scoville & Gates
Scoville, William H., machinist
Scranton, Noah, block and pump maker, cor. North State and
    North Water sts
Scranton, jr., Noah, block and pump maker, Noah Scranton
Seeley, George, saloon and boarding-house, South Water st
Seger, Joseph, waterman, Chicago avenue near Pearsons street?
Selkrig, James, clerk, Smith J. Sherwood
Sensor, John W., carpenter, Cruver & Sensor
Sexton, Stephen, carpenter, Kinzie street near North State
Seymour, Jesse, Sauganash Hotel, Market st cor. Lake
Shaddle, Peter, upholsterer, Clark street
Shapley, Morgan L., Government works, near the Garrison
Shelby, Capt. Daniel, boarding house, North Water st
Sheldon, Philo C., (Church & Sheldon)
Sheldon, C. P., clerk, Church & Sheldon
Shelley, Geo. E., Lake House, cor. North Water and Rush sts
Sheppard, Robert, carpenter and builder, Cass street near Ohio
Sheppard, ——, boarding-house, 15 Clark street
Shergold, Thomas, house and sign painter, Dearborn st
Sherman, Alanson S., mason, cor. W. Washington and Clinton
Sherman, Charles C., hostler, Mansion House
Sherman, Ezra L., teller, Illinois State Bank Branch, LaSalle st
Sherman, Francis C., contractor and builder, 85 Clark st
Sherman, Francis T., clerk, Francis C. Sherman
Sherman, Joel Sterling, farmer, Northfield
Sherman, Nathaniel, jr., Sherman & Parsons
Sherman (Oren) & Pitkin, fancy dry goods, 150 Lake street
Sherman, Silas W., ex-sheriff, 48 Clark street
Sherratt, Thomas, saloon, South Water street
Sherry, Thomas, clerk, Ira B. Eddy & Co.
Sherwood, Smith J., watchmaker and jeweller, 144 Lake st
Shields, Joseph, watch and clock repairer, Dearborn st
Shilletto, John, soap and candle maker, 3d ward
Shotwell, Henry R., Smead, Kendall & Co.
Shrigley, John, tavern keeper,
Simons, Edward, butcher, Archibald Clybourn
Sinclair, Lewis G., Parisian dyer and scourer, North Water st
Sinclair, James, tinsmith, 58 Washington street
Skinner, Charles, clerk, Mansion House
Skinner, Mark, attorney and counsellor, Clark st cor. Lake
Sloan, Charles, bricklayer, LaSalle street near Illinois
Sloan, Edward, candle maker
Smale, Samuel, stair-builder,
Smead, H. A., Smead, Kendall & Co.

Smead, Kendall & Co., ready-made clothing, 106 Lake street
Smith, Abiel, pressman, Chicago Democrat office
Smith, Barney, butcher, h lake shore, cor. Madison st
Smith, Benjamin, tailor, Dearborn street, cor. Washington
Smith, Bradner, carpenter, North State st
Smith, Charles C., law student, Spring & Goodrich
Smith, Christopher, milkman, State street
Smith, Dr. D. S., over Clark's drug store, cor. Lake and Clark
Smith, Elijah, merchant tailor, 48 Clark street
Smith, George W., general merchant, North Water street
Smith & Co., George, bankers, exchange brokers, 187 Lake st
Smith, Henry, (Wm. B. Ogden)
Smith, Hiram B., tinsmith, Wm. Wheeler
Smith & Co., James A., hat and cap manufacturers, 127 Lake st
Smith, James M., constable, Lake street
Smith, John E., clerk, Sherman & Pitkin
Smith, John M., James A. Smith & Co., 127 Lake street
Smith, John L., clerk,
Smith, Dr. John Mark, Harmon & Loomis's store
Smith, Joseph F., clerk, Mansion House
Smith, Marcellus B., clerk,
Smith, Orson, compositor, Chicago Democrat
Smith, S. Lisle, City attorney, 107 Lake st
Smith, Theophilus W., judge Supreme Court, bds. City Hotel
Smith, W. W., clerk, S. J. Surdam
Smith, William, teamster, Adams st. bet. State and Dearborn
Snell, William O., ship smith, North Water street
Snow & Co., Geo. W., lumber merchants, South Water st
Snow, Ira, teamster, Wells street
Snowhook, Wm. B., canal sub-contractor
Soden, William, farmer
Sollett, John, carpenter, with Updike & McClure
Soraghan, Daniel, teamster, Michigan street near Clark
Soraghan, John, teamster, North Water street near N. LaSalle
Spafford, J., tinsmith, Botsford & Beers
Spar, Andrew, stone mason, Rush street near Chicago avenue
Spaulding, Frank, bartender, "Eagle," 10 Dearborn street
Spaulding, John, carpenter and joiner
Speer, Isaac, watchmaker, with S. J. Sherwood
Spence, John C., hatter, 19 Clark st
Spence, James, canal contractor, 17 Clark street
Spencer, Thomas, carpenter, 135 Dearborn street
Sprague, Orlando, gunsmith, Lake street
Spring, Giles, attorney and counsellor at law, 107 Lake st
Staffen, Nicholas, laborer,
Stanton, Charles T., auctioneer, Stanton & Black
Stanton, Daniel D., Giles Williams & Co.
Stanton & Black, auctioneers and commission, 85 Lake street
State Bank Branch, LaSalle st, near South Water st
Starkweather, Chas. R., assist.-postmaster, P.O., 37 Clark st
Stearns & Hallam, fancy dry goods merchants, 148 Lake st
Stearns, Marcus C., Stearns & Hallam
Steel, George, canal contractor
Steele, Ashbel, mason builder, 3d ward

Steele, J. W., City Refectory, 15 Dearborn st
Stephenson, Capt. Godfrey, capitalist, bds Lake House
Stevenson, Capt. Chas.
Stevens, George F., drayman, South Water st
Stevens, M. W., Graves & Stevens
Stevens, Samuel, clerk
Stevens, Wm. M., light-house keeper, River street
Stewart, Ephriam T., canal contractor
Stewart, Hart L., canal contractor
Stewart, Capt. John, steamer Michigan
Stewart, Royal, attorney at law, Lake street
Stocking, Rev. S. H., Methodist church, Washington cor. Clark
Stocking, Capt. schooner Jefferson, bds. Shakespeare
Stockwell, George, laborer, South Water street
Stone, Horatio O., groceries and provisions, South Water street
* Stone, John, wood-chopper,
Storms, Abram, carpenter and builder, State street
Storkey, George, cattle dealer,
Stose (Clemens) & White (—.), blacksmiths, Randolph nr Wells
Stow, Edward, portrait painter, Lake street
Stow, Henry M., iron merchant, 11 and 13 Clark street
Stow, William H., foundry, West Randolph street
Stowell, E. C., stage-coach ticket agent, 123 Lake street
St. Palais, Maurice de, Catholic priest, nr cor. Wells & Randolph
Strachan (A.) & Scott, (W.) bankers, etc., 189 Lake street
Strail, Isaac, hardware, etc., Osbourn & Strail
Strail, J. Milo, clerk, Osbourn & Strail
Stratton, Homer, blacksmith, Asahel Pierce
Strausel, Martin, boot and shoe maker, LaSalle street
Strode, James M., register land office, Saloon Building, Clark st
Stuart, Dr. J. Jay, Rush st, opposite the Lake House
Stuart, Wm., publisher and editor of *Chicago Daily American*,
    cor. So. Water and Clark sts
Stuart, Alexander, pressman, Daily American office
Sturtevant, Austin D., school-teacher
Sturtevant, Noah, painter
Sullivan, A., actor, Chicago Theatre
Sullivan, Jeremiah H., canal sub-contractor
Sullivan, Owen, blacksmith, Dearborn street
Sulzer, Andrew, brewer, cor. Pine street and Chicago ave
Sulzer, Conrad, gardener, Lake View
Sulzer, Frederick, florist and nurseryman, Lake View
Surdam, Samuel J., dry goods, etc., 136 Lake st
Swain, Philip, coppersmith, William Wheeler & Co.
Sweeney, John, canal contractor, cor. Kinzie and N. Franklin
Sweeny, John, carpenter, bds. Henry Goodrich
Sweet, C., grocery and provision store, North Water st
Sweetser, J. Oldham, dentist, Rush st. opposite Lake House
Swift, Richard K., pawnbroker, 100 Lake st

Talcott, Edward B., United States Marshal

---

* Executed for the murder of Mrs. Thompson, July 10, 1840, near the
south-west cor. of 29th street and South Park ave. ½ mile west of the Lake.

Talcott, Mancel, farmer, Milwaukee ave
Talley, Alfred M., compositor, Chicago Democrat office
Tallmadge, S. W., boot and shoe maker, W. H. Adams
Tastaven, Basil, carpenter, bds 141 Randolph street
Tastaven, Peter, carpenter, bds 141 Randolph street
Tatham, Charles B., clerk,
Taylor, Andrew, blacksmith, William Harman
Taylor, Anson H., general supply store, near the Garrison
Taylor, Augustin Deodat, carpenter and builder, 74 Lake st
Taylor, Charles, tailor, Clark street
Taylor, Charles H., tailor, Francis H. Taylor
Taylor, Daniel, boot and shoemaker, 120 Lake st
Taylor, Deodat, carpenter, A. D. Taylor
Taylor, Col. Edmund D., Taylor, Breese Co., Lake street
Taylor, Ezra, Henry Wolcott's boarding-house
Taylor, Francis H., tailor, Wolf Point
Taylor, Francis, tailor, Francis H. Taylor
Taylor, George, tailor, Francis H. Taylor
Taylor, Ithream, blacksmith and horse shoer, Randolph street
Taylor, John, grocery and ship stores, West Water near Randoph
Taylor, L. D., at Augustin D. Taylor's
Taylor, Reuben, teamster, Monroe street near Market st
Taylor, Solomon, boot and shoe maker, Lake st
Taylor, William, compositor, Daily American office
Taylor, William H., (Dan. Taylor)
Taylor, Breese & Co., dry goods, etc., Lake street near Clark
Temple, Dr. John T., 218 Lake st
Temple, Dr. Peter, real estate agent, block 17, School Section
Tew, Prof. Geo. C., phrenologist, Cass street near Illinois
Thatcher, David C., gunsmith, Peacock & Thatcher
Thirds, William, carpenter and builder,
Thomas, William, carpenter and joiner
Thompson, Oliver H., dry goods and groceries, 102 Lake street
Tiernan, Hugh, head-waiter, Mansion House
Timoney, John, laborer, North Water street near LaSalle
Timoney, Patrick, laborer, bds James Carney
Tinkham, Edward L., cashier, (George Smith & Co.)
Titus, ———, tavern-keeper, Murphy & Titus
Töreson, Holstein, gardener, Walter L. Newberry
Towner, Norman K., clerk, Newberry & Dole
Trader, James, attorney at law, Saloon Buildings, Clark street
Trader, Moses, tavern-keeper, cor. South Water and LaSalle sts
Tripp, Robinson, carpenter, 119 Clark street
Troop, B., hats, caps, etc., New York House, 180 Lake street
Trumbull, James, dry goods jobber, at James A. Marshall's
Trowbridge, Samuel G., mail contractor, Clark street
Tucker, Henry, Dodge & Tucker
Tucker, Thomas E., cooper, South Water street
Tupper, Chester, house-mover, 46 Dearborn street
Turner, Charles, hostler, John and Leighton Turner
Turner, John and Leighton, livery stables, cor. North State and Kinzie streets
Turner, Capt. John M., Milwaukee ave near Chicago ave
Turney, Gen. James, attorney,

Tuttle, Frederick, mail contractor, Michigan City and Chicago
Tuttle, Lucius G., clerk, post-office, 37 Clark street
Tuttle, Nelson, stage agent, 180 Lake st
Twitchell, Theodore, carpenter, North State street near Kinzie
Tyler, Elmer, tailor, up stairs, 101 Lake st

Underhill, D. H., meat market, Lake street near Dearborn
Underwood, John M., bookkeeper, Kinzie & Hunter
Updike (Peter L.) & McClure (Andrew), carpenters and builders,
    (Court Place) Dearborn st

Vail, Walter, Kendall, Vail & Co., 119 Lake street
Vanderburg, D., horse-dealer, bds Randolph st. nr. Dearborn
Vandercook, Charles R., clerk, Botsford & Beers
VanOsdel, John M., contractor and builder, cor. North State
    and Kinzie sts
VanOsdel, Jesse R., carpenter, John M. VanOsdel
VanOsdel, Wm. Clark, carpenter, North Water street near State
Vassett, George, laborer,
Vaughan, William & D., clothes brokers, 159 Lake street
Vibbard & Tripp, dry goods, etc., Lake street
Villiard, L. N., grocery and provision store, 187½ Lake st
Vogt, John, bricklayer, cor. Cass and Pearsons streets
Voisar, Germain, laborer, bds Joseph Willemin

Wadhams, Carlton, milkman, Wooster & Wadhams
Wadhams, Seth, clerk, bds. Illinois Exchange
Wadsworth, Elisha, dry goods, Lake street
Wadsworth, Julius, agent, Hartford Insurance Co., 105 Lake st
Wait, H. M., grocery and provision store, Lake st
Wait, William, blacksmith,
Wakeman, Samuel, school-teacher, West Lake st. nr. N. Canal
Walker & Co., Charles, grocers and provision merchants, South
    Water st, near State
Walker, Almond, (Charles Walker & Co.)
Walker, Francis, attorney, bds. Ebenezer Peck
Walker, Joel H., bds. City Hotel
Walker, Martin O., mail contractor, (Frink & Walker) 123 Lake
Wallace, John S., canal contractor
Waller, Virgil, lumber dealer, River street
Walter, Casper, grocer and saloon, Clark street, near the ferry
Walter, Joel C., (H. Norton & Co.)
Walter, Ethan, grocer, Dearborn street
Walter, Victor, tailor
Walton, Nelson C., grocer and provision store, North Water st
Wandall, John, Great Western (variety store), 152½ Lake st
Ward, Bradish, clerk, James A. Marshall
Ward, Henry, brickmaker, Superior street, near the River
Warbreton, William, carpenter,
Ward, Bernard, teamster, 5th ward
Ware, Joseph, engraver, Clark street near South Water
Warner, Samuel M., grocer, Lake st. bet LaSalle and Wells
Warner, Seth P., clerk, Charles Walker & Co., South Water st
Warner, Spencer, carpenter, 201 Wabash ave

Warner, Wm., fanning-mill maker, Jas. V. Dickey
Warren, William, comedian, Chicago Theatre
Wasenden, Soarth, ship carpenter, LaSalle street
Watkins, Thomas, clerk, Post-office
Watkins, Charles, carpenter
Waters, Benjamin, carpenter,
Watson, A. Lansing, carpenter
Wayman, Samuel, painter, (Wayman & Dimmick)
Wayman, William, wagonmaker, Randolph street near Franklin
Wayman, Wm., house and sign painter, Franklin st
Webber, Henry, gardener, Cass street cor. White
Webster, Thomas, banker, (Geo. Smith & Co.)
Webster & Boggs, carpenters and builders, State cor. VanBuren
Weiss, Frederick, baker, John Pfund
Weir, John B., cabinet and chair maker, 184 Lake st
Welch, John, farmer, South Branch, north of 22d street
Welch, Patrick, farmer, South Branch, north of 22d street
Weller, George, teamster,
Weller, John, teamster,
Wellington, E. F., gamboleer, Randolph street near State
Wells, H. G., grocery and provision store, 101 Lake st
Wells, Seth, (chess player), bds Lake House
Wells, Wm., plasterer, bds. Buffalo Hotel, South Water street
Wentworth, John, editor and publisher of *Chicago Democrat*, 107
    Lake st
Wesencraft, Chas., carpenter and wagonmaker, Clinton c. Monroe
Wesencraft, William, painter, cor. Clinton and Monroe street
West, James, waterman, Michigan st, bt. Rush and Pine
West, Thomas, waterman, Illinois st cor. Pine
Westcott, Capt., 6th ward
Wetherell, J. B., real estate dealer, bds Tremont House
Wheeler, A. B., cigar manufacturer, Dearborn street near Lake
Wheeler, George, real estate dealer, North Dearborn street
Wheeler, Russell E., Wheeler & Peck
Wheeler, W. F., dry goods merchant, 107 Lake st.
Wheeler & Co., Wm., tin, sheet-iron, and coppersmith, 145 Lake
Wheeler & Peck, wholesale liquor dealers, Dearborn street
Wheelock, O. L., carpenter, A. Storms
Whitbeck, Henry, blacksmith, Asahel Pierce, Market street
Whitcomb, Lot, real estate dealer,
Whitney, James M., blacksmith, Asahel Pierce
White, Alex., house, sign, and ornamental painter, N. Water
    st near North Dearborn
White, Christopher, teamster, William Lill
White, George, carpenter, North Canal street near West Lake
White, George, City Crier, Market st, or at Stanton & Black's
White, Marcus L., merchant
Whiting, Sam., mate steamer St. Louis
Whiting, J. Tallman, clerk, Wm. L. Whiting
Whiting, Wm. L., produce and commission merchant, Hub-
    bard & Co.'s warehouse, North Water st near Rush
Whitlock, Thomas, boot and shoe maker, 104 Lake st
Wicker, Charles G., groceries, 87 Lake st., (J. H. & C. G. W.)
Wicker, Joel H., groceries, etc., 87 Lake street

3

Wickwire, Capt. William, schooner Minerva Smith
Wiggins, William, carpenter, North Water street
Wilcox, Leonard, gunsmith, Lake street
Wilde, Moloney & Co., dry goods, etc., South Water street
Wilde, George W., dry goods, Wilde, Moloney & Co.
Wilder, Col. Benj., contractor, Clark st, south of Twelfth
Wilcox, Leonard, gunsmith, Peacock & Thatcher
Wilkinson, Elias R., (T. B. Carter & Co.)
Willard, Alonzo J., teamster, bds Vermont House
Willard, Dr. Simeon, State street cor. of Washington
Willemin, Joseph, blacksmith, 141 Randolph street
Williams, Kiel, laborer, cor. Oak and Rush street
Williams, Eli B., Recorder, cor. Clark and Randolph sts, and
    groceries, etc., South Water st, bet Dearborn and State sts
Williams & Co., Giles, groceries, salt, etc., South Water street
Williams, Giles, Stow & Williams
Williams, J., haircutting and shaving-shop, 90 Lake st
Wills, Solomon, clerk, Circuit Court Clerk's office
Wilson, Benj. M., hardware, etc., North Water street
Wilson, John C., grocer, North Clark st. alderman, 5th ward
Wilson, John L., on the canal
Wilson, John M., attorney at law, Michigan ave
Wilson, Joseph, farmer, Arch. Clybourn
Wilson, Richard L., canal contractor, on the canal
Winchell, Sylvester, teamster, Michigan ave.
Winship, Joseph, bread and biscuit baker, South Water street
Wolcott, Alex., clerk Steamer Geo. W. Dole, for St. Joseph
Wolcott, Edward, druggist, L. M. Boyce
Wolcott, Henry H., clerk, W. L. Whiting
Wolcott, Henry, private boarding house, cor. North State and
    Kinzie sts
Wolf, Andrew,
Wood, Alonzo C., mason builder, Cass street near Ohio
Wood, Dr., 159 Lake street
Woodbury, Adoniram Judson, bookkeeper, George W. Snow
Woodbury, Hiram, clerk, bds Mrs. Woodbury
Woodville, N. D., printer, Chicago American office
Woodworth, Robert P. & James H., wholesale dry goods mer-
    chants, 103 Lake st
Wooster, (D. N.) & Wadhams, (Carlton,) milkmen, Michigan
    avenue near 14th street
Worthingham, William, plasterer, Adams st near Clark
Wraight, Thomas, gardener, block c. Desplaines & Washington
Wright, Edward, Michigan ave. cor. Madison
Wright, John, Michigan ave. cor. Madison st
Wright, John S., forwarding commission-merchant, N. Water st
Wright, Timothy, Michigan ave. cor. Madison st
Wright, Truman G., speculator, bds Tremont House
Wright, Walter, Michigan ave. cor. Madison st
Wright, Winthrop,

Yates, Horace H., grocery and provision store, 39 Clark st
Yoe, Peter L., bookkeeper, Walter S. Gurnee
Young, ————, blacksmith, Randolph street, near Clark

CHURCHES.

Baptist Church, Rev. I. T. Hinton, LaSalle st, nr. Washington.
Catholic Church, Lake st, cor. State. Rev. Timothy O'Meara.
Methodist Church, Rev. S. H. Stocking, Washington st cor Clark
Presbyterian Church, Rev. F. Bascom, Clark st, nr Washington.
St. James' Episcopal Church, Cass st, cor. Illinois. Isaac W. Hallam, rector.
First Unitarian Church, City Saloon, cor. Clark and Lake sts. Rev. Joseph Harrington, pastor.

HOTELS.

Chicago Hotel, cor. West Lake and Canal sts
Chicago Temperance House, LaSalle near Lake street
City Hotel, N.-W. cor. Clark and Randolph sts
Columbian House, Wells st cor. South Water
Illinois Exchange, 192 Lake st cor. Wells
Lake House, cor. Rush and North Water sts
Lake Street Coffee House, 141 Lake st
Mansion House, 88 Lake st
New York House, 184 Lake st
Sauganash Hotel, Market st, cor. Lake st
Shakespeare, cor. Kinzie and Rush streets
Southern Hotel, cor. State and Twelfth sts
* Tremont House, n.-w. cor. Lake and Dearborn sts
United States Hotel, West Water st cor. West Randolph
Western Hotel, cor. West Randolph and Canal streets

Circuit Clerk's office, N.-E. cor. of Public Square
Recorder's office, N.-E. cor. of Public Square
Jail and Sheriff's office, N.-W. cor. of Public Square
Post office, 37 Clark street, Saloon Buildings
U.S. Garrison, north end of Michigan ave., on the river
U.S. Light House, cor. River st, (at Rush st bridge)
U.S. Land Office Receiver, Eli S. Prescott, 177 Lake street
U.S. Land Office Register, Jas. M. Strode, over 37 Clark st
Chicago Theatre, 8 and 10 Dearborn street
Saloon Buildings, South-East corner of Lake and Clark sts
Chicago Lyceum, Grant Goodrich, Pres't, Saloon Buildings
Tippecanoe Hall, (Whig,) n.-e. cor. North State and Kinzie sts
Egan Row, Dearborn street, south of Tremont House
Blanchard Row, Washington st, So. bet. LaSalle and Wells sts
Dutch Settlement, north of Chicago ave. and east of Clark st

* Destroyed by fire, and 12 adjoining buildings, on Sunday morning, at 1 o'clock, Oct. 27th, 1839. Ira Couch, proprietor.

CITY REGISTER.

MAYOR—BENJAMIN W. RAYMOND.

ALDERMEN—

First Ward.

James A. Smith, | Oliver H. Thompson.

Second Ward.

Eli S. Prescott, | Clemens C. Stose.

Third Ward.

William H. Stow, | Ira Miltimore.

Fourth Ward.

John Murphy, | Asahel Pierce.

Fifth Ward.

Henry L. Rucker, | John C. Wilson.

Sixth Ward.

John H. Kinzie, | Buckner S. Morris.

CORPORATION NEWSPAPER—Daily American.

HIGH CONSTABLE—Samuel J. Lowe.

ASSESSORS—First Ward, Alvin Calhoun; Second Ward, Thos. Brock; Third Ward, Thos. C. James; Fourth Ward, John Gray; Fifth Ward, James Duffy; Sixth Ward, Jacob Raynor.

CHIEF ENGINEER—Alvin Calhoun; Assistant-Engineers—Charles T. Stanton and George Chacksfield.

CITY CLERK—Wm. W. Brackett.

COLLECTOR—Erastus Bowen.

TREASURER—George W. Dole.

STREET COMMISSIONER—Charles M. Gray.

CITY ATTORNEY—S. Lisle Smith.

CITY PHYSICIAN—Charles V. Dyer.

CITY SURVEYOR—Asa F. Bradley.

SEALER OF WEIGHTS AND MEASURES—George Davis.

SCHOOL INSPECTORS— Peter Bolles, David Moore, John Scott, Daniel Elston, J. Y. Scammon, Wm. H. Brown, Nathan H. Bolles.

POLICE CONSTABLES—Samuel J. Lowe, Daniel B. Heartt, D. C. Allen, George M. Huntoon.

FIRE WARDENS—First Ward, N. H. Bolles; Second Ward, Jeremiah Price; Third Ward, John Gray; Fourth Ward, John Miller; Fifth Ward, David Moore; Sixth Ward, Alonzo Wood.

BOARD OF HEALTH—Drs. Brainard, Gay, and Betts.

MAYORS OF THE CITY OF CHICAGO.

City incorporated, March, 1837.

1837 William B. Ogden.	1853 Charles M. Gray.
1838 Buckner S. Morris.	1854 Isaac L. Milliken.
1839 Benjamin W. Raymond.	1855 Levi D. Boone.
1840 Alexander Loyd.	1856 Thomas Dyer.
1841 Francis C. Sherman.	1857 John Wentworth.
1842 Benjamin W. Raymond.	1858 John C. Haines.
1843 Augustus Garrett.	1859 John C. Haines.
1844 Alanson S. Sherman.	1860 John Wentworth.
1845 Augustus Garrett.	1861 Julian S. Rumsey.
1846 John P. Chapin.	1862 Francis C. Sherman.
1847 James Curtiss	1864 Francis C. Sherman.
1848 James H. Woodworth.	1865 John B. Rice.
1849 James H. Woodworth.	1867 John B. Rice.
1850 James Curtiss.	1869 Roswell B. Mason.
1851 Walter S. Gurnee.	1871 Joseph Medill.
1852 Walter S. Gurnee.	1873 Harvey D. Colvin.

SHERIFFS OF COOK COUNTY.

County organized, 1831.

1831 James Kinzie.	officio Sheriff, from April 28th, 1855, to Nov., 1856.
1832 Stephen Forbes.	
1834 Silas W. Sherman.	1856 John L. Wilson.
1836 Silas W. Sherman.	1858 John Gray.
1838 Isaac R. Gavin.	1860 Anthony C. Hesing.
1840 Ashbel Steele.	1862 David Hammond.
1842 Samuel J. Lowe.	1864 John A. Nelson.
1844 Samuel J. Lowe.	1866 John L. Beveridge.
1846 Isaac Cook.	1868 Gustav Fischer.
1848 Isaac Cook.	Benj. L. Cleaves, Coroner, and ex- officio Sheriff, from April 15th, 1870, to Nov., 1870.
1850 William L. Church.	
1852 Cyrus P. Bradley.	1870 Timothy M. Bradley.
1854 James Andrew.	1872 Timothy M. Bradley.
James S. Beach, Coroner, and ex-	1874 Francis Agnew.

CHARTER ELECTION, MAY 2, '37.

WHIG TICKET.
ANTI-CAUCUS CANDIDATES.

For Mayor:

JOHN H. KINZIE.

For High-Constable:

ALVIN CALHOUN.

For Aldermen:

1st Ward—CHAS. L. HARMON, GILES SPRING.
2d   "   —GEO. W. DOLE, THOMAS BROCK.
4th   "   —ALEX. LOGAN, JOHN C. HUGUNIN.
6th   "   —JOHN B. F. RUSSELL, NELSON R. NORTON.

For Assessors:

1st Ward—ERASTUS BOWEN.   4th Ward—WM. FORSYTH.
2d   "   —JEREMIAH PRICE.   6th   "   —AMOS C. HAMILTON.

DEMOCRATIC TICKET. (Elected.)

For Mayor:

WILLIAM B. OGDEN.

For High-Constable:

JOHN SHRIGLEY.

For Aldermen:

1st Ward—J. C. GOODHUE, F. C. SHERMAN.
2d   "   —PETER BOLLES, JOHN S. C. HOGAN.
3d   "   —JOHN DEAN CATON.
4th   "   —ASAHEL PIERCE, FRANCIS H. TAYLOR.
5th   "   —BERNARD WARD.
6th   "   —SAMUEL JACKSON, HIRAM PEARSONS.

For Assessors:

[The names of the Assessors cannot be found.]

POLLING PLACES:

1st WARD—"Eagle," No. 10 Dearborn Street.
2d   "   —Lincoln Coffee House.
3d   "   —Chas. Taylor's House, Canal Street.
4th   "   —Chicago Hotel (Cox's), N.-E. cor. N. Canal and
                W. Lake Streets.
5th   "   —Canal Office, N. Water Street,
6th   "   —Franklin House (Eachus & Dennis), N. Water St.

JUDGES OF ELECTION.

1st WARD—Wilson McClintock, E. H. Hadduck, F. C. Sherman·
2d   "   —Alex. Loyd, P. F. W. Peck, Geo. W. Dole.
3d   "   —Ashbel Steele, Charles Taylor, Geo. Vardon.
4th   "   —David Cox, John C. Hugunin, F. A. Howe.
5th   "   —Joel Manning, Patrick Murphy, Bemsley Huntoon.
6th   "   —Gholson Kercheval, J. H. Kinzie, E. S. Kimberly.

FIRST ELECTION

IN THE

CITY OF CHICAGO

FOR MAYOR.

TUESDAY, MAY 2, 1837.

FIRST WARD.

FOR WILLIAM B. OGDEN:

Sidney Abel,
Isaac N. Arnold,
Bennett Bailey,
H. Bailey, *sworn*,
Pat'k Ballingall,
Medor B. Beaubien,
Samuel C. Bennett,
Nathan H. Bolles
John Calhoun,
Henry B. Clarke,
J. H. Coffin,
Peter Cohen,
F. G. Conner,
A. Jackson Cox,
J. G. Dawley,
Charles V. Dyer,
Thomas Ely,
Charles M. Gray,
Joseph H. Gray,
David P. Foot,
Jared Fordham
C. C. Franklin,
John Hackett,
Eri B. Hulbert,
Henry King,
John Knight,
David Lake,
George Lamb, *sworn*
Albert G. Leary,
W. McClintock,
Alex. McDommerly,
John Melray,
Ephriam Morrison,
Orsemus Morrison

Luther Nichols,
Peter Pruyne,
John Robson,
John Sammons,
J. Shadeller,
James Sinclair,
Barney Smith,
John Smith,
S. F. Spaulding,
Augustin D. Taylor,
Edmund D. Taylor,
Peter L. Updike,
H. C. Walker,
Anson Weed,
Slater West,
Eli B. Williams,
Wm. Worthingham,
William Jones,
W. West,
H. L. Patterson,
S. Ward,
Edward L. Thrall,
J. H. Walker,
Ambrose Burnham,
E. Gale,
J. K. Palmer,
H. Burk,
L. Morse,
Wm. Montgomery,
Alex. N. Fullerton,
J. Scott,
James M. Strode,
David S. Smith,
Alanson Follansbee,

W. Winters,
B. H. Kent,
Chester Tupper,
M. Shonts,
Daniel Miller,
James H. Collins,
John Kelly,
Joseph Adams,
Daniel McKenzie,
Ebenezer Peck,
J. Wentworth, *sworn*
E. H. Mulford,
Daniel Brainard,
W. Andrews,
Enoch Plummer,
J. C. Goodhue,
H. Harrington,
Robinson Tripp,
Ira Couch,
John Wright,
C. W. Spafford,
Francis C. Sherman,
John Boyd,
Hiram B. Smith,
M. O'Connor,
J. F. Brown,
A. J. Luce,
David Carver,
J. M. Smith,
L. F. Lewis,
John R. Livingston,
B. F. Monroe,
John Patterson,
Colon Ware.

FOR JOHN H. KINZIE:

L. C. P. Freer,   Thomas A. Clark,   F. A. Harding,
T. O. Davis,   Royal Stewart,   Thomas T. Durant,
Alvin Calhoun,   Isaac D. Harmon,   Edward Casey,
Hiram Mallory,   Jabez K. Botsford,   George W. Merrill,
J. Young Scammon,   Parker M. Cole,   John W. Hooker,
Joseph L. Hanson,   Tyler K. Blodgett,   Charles C. Smith,
John F. Spalding,   Curtis Havens   Giles Spring,
Oliver H. Thompson,   Elijah K. Hubbard,   L. B. Goodsell
Levi D. Boone,   Ezekiel Morrison,   William Stuart
C. B. Ware,   David Gelland,   H. Terrill,
Joseph Meeker,   James A. Smith,   Charles Adams,
J. B. Wetherell,   Lorin Graves,   J. Gardner,
George W. Snow,   David Hatch,   Alva V. Frasier,
James H. Rees,   Cyrenus Beers,   Edw. H. Haddock,
H. Markoe,   Simeon Loveland,   Frederick A. Howe,
William Bond,   Seth Paine,   A. Nobles,
Robert Truman,   Samuel C. Dennis,   E. S. Hopkins,
James Spence,   Erastus Bowen,   Charles McClure,
Heman Bond,   W. K. Marchal,   S. Willis Grannis,
P. Balcom,   John L. Wilson,   Dexter Graves,
J. Sharp,   Thomas Wright,   Edward Colvin.
W. Finney,   M. Ayres,

SECOND WARD.

FOR WILLIAM B. OGDEN:

Solomon Lincoln   Mich'l Fitzsimmons   A. H. Beard
Henry Rhines   M. Castigen   A. Grusgutt
Samuel J. Lowe   Samuel Carpenter   James O'Brien
Thomas Marr   P. Groover   Daniel Levinney
Russell Wheeler   John Perian   H. Duffey
Peter Bolles   Godford Stevens   J. Beach
C. McWhorter   H. McCarley   Eli S. Prescott
S. S. Bradley   M. Fisher   J. Walker
Daniel B. Heartt   B. Miglog   John C. Rue
Charles P. Hogan   Hiram Hugunin   Chas. H. Chapman
P. Higgins   Samuel Wayman   Moses Dutton
J. C. Hibson   Benj. Briggs   Valentine A. Boyer
W. Devere   Joseph Peacock   P. J. Kimball
J. Spencer   P. McConnel   J. Sweeney
Michael Glen   F. C. Tupper   D. Conley
Silas W. Sherman   J. Norris   D. Crawley
Richard Murphy   James A. Merrie   R. Halney
F. C. Bold   H. Mitchell   John Lang
John Larry   A. Coop   Alexander Loyd
J. Outhet   Geo. E. Horehart   E. E. Hunter
J. O'Rourke   M. Croushong   Michael Frarey
T. Watkins   E. Lelley   James Carney
J. McCormick   J. Lane   Thomas Farlin
J. J. Kinnon   T. C. Sampson   Augustus H. Burley
McKelley   Wm. Alamhart   A. Brigg
John Sarlney   D. Denney   S. J. Graves
John Campton   H. Brown   —. McDalald

John Sennet
John Dunlap
Louis Malzacher
Stephen M. Edgel
William Wiggins
John Mitchell
Dennis S. Dewey
A. Tholser
T. Bailey
Edmund Gill
Martin Stidel
Samuel J. Grannis
V. McIntire
W. M. Hartley
C. Longwood
J. Dailey
O. Brian
Peter Casey
A. Berg
John Ashman
B. Peck
T. Lacey
George Bryan
P. Whitmore
Robert Garner
Joseph Shields
R. Jones
Clemens Stose
J. Funk
A. Panakaske
Edward Manierre
Wm. Hague
John H. Butler

J. M. Hammond
M. Nigle
Alonzo Huntington
Edward Dimmock
Wm. Jinkins
Isaac R. Gavin
A. Bailey
P. J. Duncan
T. Fox
J. McCord
J. Sullivan
A. Duckman
J. Gluwater
O. Sheppheard
F. Goodman
D. Harsem
C. Culshaw
John W. Eldridge
Wm. B. French
Simon Cooley
John Ryan
Michael Buck
T. O. Maley
Fra's G. Blanchard
John K. Boyer
John Knight
J. Dickson
James Lenon
John Archdale
M. Sanduskey
Robert Hart
John Dillon

J. P. Johnston
P. Donahue
John Rice
Peter Shaddle
L. F. Monroe
Jacob Gramos
J. J. Jones
Peter Dolesey
John Woodhouse
Jacob Milemin
C. Benedict
Joseph Winship
John Shrigley
— O. Mahan
Thos. Wolfinger
S. B. Dane
E. F. Brown
N. Winslow
John Gormonly
George Dolton
J. Minney
Michael Lantry
S. Hurley
John Murphey
P. Kelley
John Black
Wm. B. Noble'
Thomas Ghan
C. De Wier
H. Bird
J. C. Gauck
P. Rogers

FOR JOHN H. KINZIE:

John M. Turner
Star Foot
L. T. Howard
Abraham Gale
— Butler
George Patterson
Silas B. Cobb
S. C. George
Joseph N. Balestier
William Truman
J. F. T. Libb
John Jay Stuart
Smith J. Sherwood
W. Haskins
Philo Carpenter
H. L. Roberts
Arthur G. Burley
H. Zalle
P. S. Smith
John Pomeroy

F. D. Marshall
Thomas Hamilton
L. Johnston
C. Walter
O. Sprague
Tuthill King
J. McLabban
George W. Dole
R. Price
James Rockwell
John P. Cook
John Dolesey
Francis Walker
Jeremiah Price
M. Smith
J. Briggs
E. S. Hobbie
C. Murphy
John Casey
P. F. W. Peck

George Law
A. S. Bates
T. Jenkins
R. Drummond
E. Simons
James O. Humphrey
Abram F. Clarke
H. H. Magee
A. Hatch
P. J. Monroe
W. H. Clarke
T. C. Tucker
T. S. Hide
John P. Chapin
James White
John Dei
M. Dunning
A. D. Higgins
Thomas Brock
Benj. W. Raymond

THIRD WARD.

FOR WILLIAM B. OGDEN:

Samuel Southerden	Morris O. Jones	Lewis P. Dekart
Oliver Lozier	George Vardon	L. C. Hugunin
Hamilton Barnes	S. E. Downer	Mitchell Ferryark
Thomas James	William Mitchell	George Chacksfield
George U. Gun	John Welch	John B. Miller
Henry Walton	George Davis	John Rudiman
John B. Weir	George Brown	Joseph Wilberman
John Bates, Jr.	Patrick Welch	Joseph Calef
William H. Barber	John Mahan	Peter Sawnett
Charles Taylor	Solomon Taylor	

FOR JOHN H. KINZIE:

J. S. P. Lord	Thomas Bishop	John Gage
Ashbel Steele	David Bradley	James Crawford
Thomas Cook	Charles A. Lawber	Henry Burke

FOURTH WARD.

FOR WILLIAM B. OGDEN:

A. M. Talley	Charles Cleaver	Francis H, Taylor
J. W. Chadwick	George M. Davis	Asahel Pierce
Patrick Lane	Isaac Haight	Francis Peyton
E. F. Wellington	Samuel M. Brooks	Joel D. Howe
George Frost	William Ford	William Saltonstall
John B. Brodain	Samuel Akin	Zemos Allen
Seth P. Warner	James Wakeman	Seth Johnson
Geo. White	Edward Perkins	Philip Will
Homer Stratton	J. W. Titus	Alford Allen
A. Chapron	Jas. Mathews	Lucien Peyton
John Welmaher	A. S. Sherman	N. Christia
Christian Astah	John C. Hugunin	George Hays
Thomas Oak	P. E. Cassaday	Frederick A. Howe
Stephen Harrel	Alexander Logan	James Lafrombois
James Jenkins	James M. Whitney	R. W. Hyde
William Carneyhaw	Henry Taylor	George Atterbury
Robert Marshall		

FOR JOHN H. KINZIE:

Edward Perkins	Antoine Loupean	Edward Parsons
William Forsyth	John Ludby	James Kinzie
Francis Chapron	Daniel Elston	David Cox
Marshall Cornair		

FIFTH WARD.

FOR WILLIAM B. OGDEN:

John Dunehen	John Hart	J. Eddy
John Coats	John Lenay	J. McCue
John Wilson	J. W. Donnell	J. McLaughlin
Joseph Kent	A. Gartley	B. Adouy
Bryan Curley	B. Cain	P. Grodavent

P. Scott
M. Spelman
T. Midery
Wm. Fowls
P. Conlen
P. Finney
P. Murphy
H. Galloughent
T. Weed
T. McHale
B. Ward
T. Gormoniley
A. Sullivan
M. Burk
P. Ackles

T. Farrell
E. Gibbins
T. McNamara
P. Monaghen
T. Riden
M. O. Midloy
T. Brown
Henry Cunningham
E. B. Talcott
M. Baumgarten
G. Peyton
S. Dougan
J. Seymour
J. Mallady

T. Hughes
T. Carrall
W. Bell
D. Moore
H. Frye
J. Breadman
J. D. Oddman
H. Harmer
J. Connolley
J. King
L. Frey
N. Thomason
P. Bartlett
T. McGee

FOR JOHN H. KINZIE:

T. Wilson

Bemsley Huntoon

SIXTH WARD.

FOR WILLIAM B. OGDEN:

James West
William Lill
P. Campbell
John Censure
E. Flosser
J. Zoliski
L. Barber
E. T. Ward
J. Kennedy
Robert Shepperd
J. M. Baxley
J. S. Wheeler
J. Godlin
J. Tracey
J. Mills
A. Hall
W. Burns
Thomas Cody
J. Miller
Pattieson Nickalls
E. N. Churchill
B. F. Hall
J. N. Hayes
Morgan Shapley
S. Gifford

Wm. V. Smith
D. Drummond
V. B. Keith
D. Bucknell
A. Hoofmin
H. A. Pardee
F. Carroll
John Turner
G. Pardee
F. Freeman
J. Tornee
C. Conner
William B. Egan
Wm. Harman
N. J. Brown
P. Hadley
E. S. Kimberly
Gholson Kercheval
S. D. Pierce
E. Cammock
E. Suil
S. Jackson
L. Hunt
W. Sabine

Hiram Pearsons
John Allen
J. L. Campbell
W. Boyden
D. Ryan
J. S. Olin
S. Sexton
W. Koas
J. Whorton
W. Armstrong
J. Vanderbogert
P. Kelsey
J. Ferisu
Ralph Peck
J. Mannerlin
H. O. Stone
Thomas Carroll
P. Baumgarten
C. S. Tibbles
M. Vanderbogert
Francis Kesler
J. T. Betts
T. Sullivan
D. Calliun

FOR JOHN H. KINZIE:

Luke Wood
John N. Bronson
Charles Pettit
J. T. Callis
L. G. Osborne

James L. Howe
F. Haughton
J. Stofer
Abijah S. Perry
Isaac Legg

L. L. Cheeney
J. Grant
M. Clinton
B. D. Wheeler
Alonzo C. Wood

46 FIRST CITY ELECTION, 1837.

W. B. Plumb, J. Forcht, D. Creden
Robert A. Kinzie, A. Spoor, E. C. Brackett
B. Emerson, George Legg, J. Schrider
Chris. H. Berkinbile, T. Barnum, J. Magger
Grant Goodrich, N. R. Norton, G. Wills
Walter L. Newberry, S. Akers, J. Chandler
J. T. Hinsdale, W. Sterns, A. C. Hamilton
Lewis C. Kercheval, S. Smith, J. Soother
Josiah E. McClure, T. Shepherd, W. Anderson
John B. F. Russell, W. A. Thompson, J. Brown
T. Greenwood, Charles Harding, J. Lampman
John M. Underwood, Thomas Wilson, G. Frost
Gurdon S. Hubbard, A. Cole, P. Butler
J. Crawford, H. Warren, W. Halpin
M. Miller, S. M. Greenwood, C. F. How
S. Northrup, Henry G. Hubbard, W. Carrivan
P. Cable, J. Nesbit, E. Farr
Buckner S. Morris, C. Ford, F. German
A. Overhart, A. Hubbard

Total votes in Chicago in 1837 by wards:

First 170
Second 238
Third 38
Fourth 59
Fifth 60
Sixth 144

709

Total votes in Chicago in 1837 by divisions:

South 408
West 97
North 204

709

WARD BOUNDARIES:

FIRST—South side east of Clark street.
SECOND—South side west of Clark street to the River.
THIRD—South of West Randolph street, west of the River.
FOURTH—West of the River, north of West Randolph street.
FIFTH—North of the River, west of North Clark street.
SIXTH—North of the River, east of North Clark street.

LOTS SOLD IN FT. DEARBORN ADDITION

TO THE

TOWN OF CHICAGO,

From the 10th to the 24th of June, inclusive. Known as the
BEAUBIEN, or RESERVATION Lands.

Aggregate amount of Sales, about $100,000.

B'k.	Lot.	Bidders.	A'mt.
1		*Reserved.*	
2	1	H. Norton,	$2657
	2	"	1557
	3	A. J. Underhill,	1506
	4	"	1506
	5	L. R. Lyon,	1400
	6	"	1500
	7	George S. Smith,	1509
	8		
	9	*Reserved.*	
	10		
3	1	C. M. Reed,	2500
	2	"	2000
	3	"	2000
	4	M. D. Ogden,	2000
	5	T. Church and H. O. Stone,	1077
	6	A. Bronson,	233
	7	E. B. Hurlburt,	2100
	8	I. Cook, Jas. Turney,	4150
4	1		
	2		
	3	*Reserved.*	
	4		
	5		
	6		
	7	Thomas Webster,	206
	8	A. Bronson,	303
	9	L. R. Lyon,	150
	10	A. Bronson,	303
	11	"	303
	12	"	303
	13	"	303
	14	"	303

B'k.	Lot.	Bidders.	Am't.
	15	A. Bronson,	233
	16	"	267
	17	"	303
	18	"	333
	19	"	433
	20	"	363
	21	"	303
	22	"	583
	23	P. Strachan,	630
	24	C. Lyon,	350
	25	L. R. Lyon,	300
	26	"	250
	27	D. Brainard,	230
	28	L. R. Lyon,	250
	29	P. Fitzgibbons,	276
	30	L. R. Lyon,	325
	31	"	325
	32	Dr. H. Humphrey,	431
	33	L. R. Lyon,	400
	34	"	200
	35	P. Fitzgibbon,	265
	36	L. R. Lyon,	200
	37	P. Fitzgibbon,	262
	38	J. Burgess,	226
	39	C. Walker,	408
	40		
	41	Geo. L. Campbell,	195
	42	L. C. Kercheval,	153
	43	Geo. L. Campbell,	150
	44	John Foot,	152
5	1		
	2		
	3	*Reserved.*	
	4		
	5		

B'k.	Lot.	Bidders.	Am't.
	6	J. H. Collins,	211
	7	"	211
	8	"	210
	9	"	209
	10	"	208
	11	J. B. Beaubien,	225
6	1	D. Root,	359
	2	James Carney,	263
	3	F. C. Sherman,	163
	4	"	163
	5	John C. Gibson,	165
	6	Forfeited.	
7	1	Walter Kimball,	600
	2	"	450
	3	S. Willard,	290
	4	Thos. Dyer,	225
	5	"	225
	6	I. N. Arnold,	238
	7	Thos. Dyer,	231
	8	"	235
	9	John Ordes,	303
	10	J. H. Kinzie,	273
	11	"	207
	12	Geo. L. Campbell,	215
	13	"	215
	14	J. Russell,	215
	15	"	220
	16	"	221
	17	Geo. L. Campbell,	212
	18	E. S. Prescott,	137
	19	E. Davlin,	167
	20	J. H. Kinzie,	151
	21	A. D. Stewart,	205
	22	"	265
	23	J. Butterfield,	356
	24	"	305
	25	"	312
	26	"	315
	27	S. N. Dexter,	312
	28	R. T. Haines,	303
	29	T. King & Follansbee,	426
	30	A. D. Stewart,	351
	31	M. Ayers,	476
8	1	John Bowen,	853
	2	"	633
	3	Luke Coyne,	556
	4	Mosely & McCord,	507
	5	Chas. McDonnell,	506
	6	S. B. Collins,	477
	7	Dan Taylor,	527
	8	"	433
	9	James Carney,	450
	10	Chas. Walker,	451
	11	P. Strachan,	404
	12	Pat. Timony,	451
	13	O. H. Thompson,	503
	14	"	576
	15	"	890
	16	Charles Phelps,	610
	17	"	510
	18	"	460
	19	"	460
	20	A. G. Hobbie,	503
	21	J. Wadsworth,	466
	22	P. F. W. Peck,	511
	23	E. W. Taylor,	506
	24	N. King,	400
	25	S. B. Collins,	527
	26	Mosely & McCord,	567
	27	J. J. Phelps,	510
	28	Francis Walker,	776
	29	John Fennerty,	475
	30	S. N. Beers,	812
9	1	Stiles Burton,	712
	2	"	612
	3	"	555
	4	T. Church, jr.,	570
	5	Stiles Burton,	480
	6	S. N. Dexter,	429
	7	R. T. Haines,	455
	8	John Davlin,	406
	9	J. Wadsworth,	503
	10	S. Paine,	530
	11	S. L. Smith,	465
	12	"	495
	13	J. M. Smith,	435
	14	J. Wadsworth,	481
	15	S. L. Smith,	561
	16	John King, jr.,	257
	17	"	234
	18	"	227
	19	"	227
	20	"	212
	21	"	222
	22	"	221
	23	"	229
	24	"	237
	25	J. W. Hooker,	276
	26	T. Wheeler,	215
	27	Thos. Dyer,	217
	28	"	217
	29	"	217
	30	E. H. Haddock,	232
	31	T. Wheeler,	263
10	1	R. T. Haines,	429
	2	"	360

B'k.	Lot.	Bidders.	Am't.	B'k.	Lot.	Bidders.	Am't.
	3	R. T. Haines,	325		7	S. Willard,	401
	4	"	315		8	"	557
	5	S. N. Dexter,	305	**13**	1	J. Wadsworth,	451
	6	B. McDonald,	331		2	"	401
	7	J. H. Collins,	353		3	J. K. Botsford,	470
	8	"	353		4	"	470
	9	Isaac F. Massy.	300		5	A. G. Hobbie,	380
	10	S. B. Cobb,	268½		6	S. Willard,	376
	11	"	247½		7	J. Wadsworth,	401
	12	E. H. Haddock,	151		8	"	503
	13	"	151		9	S. Willard,	415
	14	Peter Merril,	150		10	"	403
	15	Stanton & Black,	215		11	"	376
	16	S. N. Beers,	225		12	"	362
	17	J. Russell,	231		13	"	361
	18	"	231		14	R. T. Haines,	403
	19	E. S. Prescott,	127		15	A. Wright,	480
	20	B. M. Wilson,	201		16	"	560
	21	"	193	**14**	1	J. Wadsworth,	427
	22	J. M. Underwood,	161		2	"	403
	23	J. Y. Scammon,	153		3	"	327
	24	"	205		4	F. A. Marshall,	305
	25	"	215		5	John Calhoun,	319
	26	A. D. Stewart,	230		6	J. Wadsworth,	257
	27	J. K. Botsford,	215		7	"	307
	28	J. P. Chapin,	216		8	"	327
	29	S. N. Dexter,	210		9	"	307
	30	"	210		10	"	257
	31	R. T. Haines,	203		11	"	257
	32	"	210		12	"	276
	33	J. P. Chapin,	227		13	"	317
	34	A. G. Hobbie,	305		14	"	357
11	1	J. C. Gibson,	103	**15**	1	D. P. Foot,	375
	2	A. D. Stewart,	51		2	J. Wadsworth,	317
	3	"	51		3	J. Morrison,	251
	4	"	51		4	H. O. Stone,	300
	5	T. Church, jr.,	51		5	H. A. Blakesly,	279
	6	"	51		6	J. King, jr.,	306
	7	"	51		7	J. M. Morrison,	263
	8	John Wright,	65		8	W. C. Watson, jr.,	303
12	1	S. Willard,	501		9	S. C. Clarke,	355
	2	"	401		10	Thos. Dyer,	357
	3	R. C. Bristol,	465		11	"	317
	4	"	465		12	"	307
	5	J. J. Phelps,	564		13	John King, jr.,	366
	6	R. C. Bristol,	465		14	"	412

POPULATION OF CHICAGO.

1835	3,265	1849	23,047	1863	160,000
1836	3,820	1850	28,269	1864	169,353
1837	4,179	1851	34,437	1865	178,900
1838	4,000	1852	38,733	1866	200,418
1839	4,200	1853	60,652	1867	220,000
1840	4,479	1854	65,872	1868	252,054
1841	5,752	1855	80,028	1869	273,043
1842	6,248	1856	84,113	1870	298,977
1843	7,580	1857	93,000	1871	334,270
1844	8,000	1858	90,000	1872	364,377
1845	12,088	1859	95,000	1873	465,650
1846	14,169	1860	112,172	1874	475,000
1847	16,859	1861	120,000	1875	500,000
1848	20,023	1862	138,835	1876	525,000

1885, (estimated by Jno. S. Wright,) 1,000,000.

1911, (estimated by J. N. Balestier,) 2,000,000.

"Chicago people may be excused for referring, on almost every occasion, to the greatness of our city, for its growth has become a marvel to all creation. Nothing proves the importance, absolute and relative, of the city of Chicago more than does the constant reference made to it by the rest of the world. Not a magazine paper, which has for its object the demonstration of enterprise, that does not point to Chicago; there is scarcely a modern book, be it descriptive, historical, or romantic, that does not find one or more comparisons for Chicago: the newspapers on both sides of the Atlantic have something to say in every issue about Chicago; people in the East, who feign ignorance of everything Western, always admit that they have heard remarkable things about Chicago; foreigners, who are in fact ignorant of the geography of the country and the customs of our people, know something about Chicago. * * * *
Our peculiar institutions, our unparalleled growth, our well-rewarded energy — all command respect where they do not challenge rivalry and excite envy."

PREFACE

AND

HISTORICAL SKETCH,

COMPILED FOR THE

CHICAGO DIRECTORY IN 1843.

ELLIS & FERGUS, PRINTERS AND PUBLISHERS.

THE DIRECTORY OF CHICAGO, now presented to the public, may be regarded as an experiment. It must be decided by those for whose use and benefit it has been prepared, whether it is required, and can be sustained. The sudden rise, and unexampled prosperity of Chicago, have created a curiosity in regard to its early history, and the incidents connected with its rise and progress, which considerations of interest, if nothing else, impel us to embrace every suitable opportunity to gratify. It is believed, that heretofore the sources of information have been altogether inadequate to accomplish this purpose. While the most strenuous exertions have been made, in other places, by misrepresentation and downright falsehood, in regard to our circumstances and condition, to induce emigration to stop short or to pass by us, and to divert capital and enterprise into other and foreign channels; very little or nothing has been done on our part, to remedy the evil, and disabuse the public mind abroad, of the false impressions thus engendered. Relying upon the reality which the experience of every day presents to us, of our condition—upon what we know ourselves, of the never failing sources of our prosperity, we have been comparatively indifferent in regard to the opinion of others, and blind to the effect of that opinion upon our own interest. The ignorance prevailing at the East, even in those cities with which we have the most intimate commercial relations, in regard to the size, business, and resources of Chicago, has been a matter of surprise to all whose attention has been called to the fact. The present is a most important conjuncture in our affairs. Our prospects are brightening—our harbor is nearly completed— the work on our canal shortly to be resumed—the credit of our State daily improving—and the finances of our City in a most flourishing condition. Our citizens will, we hope, forever be exempt from the burdens of heavy taxation. Never were the inducements to emigrate and settle here, greater than at the present time. It has been thought, that a Directory, containing, in addition to the matter usually introduced into such works, a brief historical and statistical account of the City, may, independent of the

4

benefit which our citizens will derive from it, in the transaction of business, be made to subserve the additional purpose of conveying to the public abroad a correct impression of the City, in almost every particular.

The utmost difficulty has been experienced, while preparing the historical and statistical parts of the work, in procuring facts and statements from authentic sources. Consequently, those parts are less full and perfect than they were originally intended to be—much less so than the author would have made them. Errors and omissions will doubtless be discovered throughout the work—no apologies, however, will be necessary to those who are acquainted with the difficulties in the way of preparing the first Directory for a new city. Such persons would probably be more surprised to find it in every respect perfect. Nothing has intentionally been left out that could add either to the interest or value of the work.

The greatest exertion has been made, to give the names of Germans and other Old Country people, correctly. Notwithstanding this, mistakes will doubtless be discovered in the orthography of these names, owing to the fact, that many are unable to spell their own names, in English. It is hoped, however, that instances of this kind will not be found to be numerous. In subsequent editions of the work the author hopes to be able to avoid them altogether, and also to give the names of such persons as are not included in this volume.

Chicago, it is to be remembered, is yet in its infancy, and subject to fluctuation in its population and business, more so than larger and older cities. So far as this is true, a Directory will be of less utility. It is believed, however, that this inconvenience is diminishing, and will be less felt hereafter. Our citizens are becoming sensible of the importance of fixed habitations and places of business,—and will speedily take measures to secure to themselves the benefits and advantages to be derived therefrom. This, to a considerable extent, has been effected the present season. Nearly three-fourths of our population will hereafter, at least for many years, be permanently located. Hoping that the book may be made in many ways to subserve a useful purpose, and prove the means of advancing, to some extent, the interest of our young but flourishing City, it is most respectfully submitted to the public. Our citizens have always been characterized for their liberality and public spirit. They will not, in this instance, forfeit their claims to this distinction, but will, generously and cheerfully, lend their aid and co-operation, to sustain an undertaking, designed to promote and advance the interests of the whole.

To those gentlemen who have encouraged the work, both as subscribers and advertisers, and those who have afforded information, and contributed their advice in furtherance of the design of the publication, the author would, in conclusion, tender his most sincere thanks.

CHICAGO, *December 1, 1843.*

HISTORICAL SKETCH.

CHICAGO, Cook County, Illinois, is situated on the south-western shore of Lake Michigan, at the head of Lake navigation, in lat. 41 deg., 45 sec., north, and long. 10 deg., 45 sec., west. The site of the city occupies a level prairie, on both sides of the main stream and the north and south branches of Chicago River, and covers an area of about three and a half miles in length, north and south, and two and a half in breadth, east and west,* about a mile and a half square of which is already regularly built upon, and the streets opened and graded. The streets are regularly laid out, parallel and at right angles to the Lake, and are wide and spacious. There are several extensive blocks of brick buildings, principally occupied as business houses and public offices, three and a half and four stories in height. The dwellings are principally of wood, many of them, however, very fine specimens of correct architecture. The portion of the city extending several miles along the shore of the Lake is sandy, and, consequently, at all seasons, dry. The portion removed from the Lake partakes of the character of all level prairie, being, in the spring and fall, wet and muddy. The site of the city, being a plain, does not afford, either from the Lake or the surrounding country, a very interesting field of vision. Chicago River and its branches, which run through the heart of the city, and admit, at all seasons, vessels of every class navigating the Lake, some distance into the interior, afford peculiar facilities for a harbor, and give to Chicago advantages, in a commercial point of view, unsurpassed by any city in the west. The Illinois and Michigan Canal, which is shortly to be completed, will add greatly to the natural advantages of Chicago, making it a principal point, and necessarily a place of transshipment on the great northern route, connecting the Atlantic States with the valley of the Mississippi. The city is bounded on the south and west by a prairie, varying from ten to twelve miles in width, some portion of which is high, and of a very superior quality. It is surrounded in every direction by a country the most productive in the world, already brought into a state of successful cultivation, and sending to its market, annually, a vast amount of produce of every description for sale, exchange for goods, or shipment, as the case may be. The climate is healthy and salubrious—as much so as any in the west. In 1837, Chicago became an incorporated city, the Act of the Legislature conferring its charter being granted and approved March 4th, of that year. The city is divided into six wards. The first and second wards, divided by Clark Street, are bounded by the south branch, Chicago River, and the Lake—the first ward lying east, and the second west of Clark Street. The third and fourth wards, divided by W. Randolph Street, are situated on the west side of the north and south branches—the third south and the fourth north of W. Randolph Street. The fifth and sixth wards, divided by N. Clark St., are bounded by the north branch, Chicago River, and the Lake—the fifth being west and the sixth east of N. Clark St. The government of the city is vested in a Common Council, composed of the Mayor and twelve Aldermen,

* In 1876, it is three and a half miles east and west, and six miles north and south.

two for each ward, all chosen annually. The Common Council, in addition to their other powers and duties, are constituted, by virtue of their office, Commissioners of Common Schools, with power to levy and collect taxes for their support, and to exercise a general supervision over matters, pertaining to them. In 1832 and the beginning of 1833, Chicago had about 100 inhabitants and five or six log houses—exclusive of the Fort and its appurtenances. In 1840, the population had increased to 4853. The present population exceeds 7580, and may be said, at this time, to amount to 8000. The period of the greatest prosperity of Chicago was from 1833 to 1837. The revulsions and reverses of '36–7 greatly retarded its growth. It continued, however, though more gradually, to increase in business and resources until '40–1, from which time business received a new impulse, and it is now enjoying a degree of prosperity equal to any former period of its history.

What the destiny of Chicago is to be the future alone can determine. Judging by the past, it seems difficult to assign a limit to its advancement. It presents, undoubtedly, one of the most remarkable instances of sudden rise to commercial importance to be found in our age. So rapid, indeed, has been its growth—with such gigantic strides has it moved onward in its career, that little space is left to mark and calculate the successive stages of its progress. We behold it, from a distant and isolated colony, inhabited only by some five or six families clinging to a lone and solitary military post for protection, and dependent for subsistence upon the uncertain arrival of some chance vessel from Mackinaw, in the short space of eight or ten years, become a mighty city, teeming with a busy and enterprising population, the centre of a widely-extending and flourishing commerce. To those who have been here from the beginning—and there are many among us—the change must be striking—the contrast between what is and what was great indeed. History, in this instance, has assumed the air of romance. Truly has a change come over the spirit of our dream. It seems difficult to reconcile to the mind that the spot, now covered with stately blocks of buildings, and alive in every direction with a busy and eager multitude, actively and profitably employed in the numerous departments of our growing commerce, was, so recently, a low and marshy plain, of which the wild beasts of the prairies were almost the solitary tenants; that but yesterday, comparatively, the wild Indian held here his council-fire, and roamed abroad unmolested in the enjoyment of his native freedom.

A country so recent as this cannot be presumed to afford very abundant materials for history. The incidents, however, connected with the rise and progress of the city, the causes which first gave it an impulse, and the works of public and domestic improvement—upon which its future prosperity depend—together with such events as transpired upon the spot at an early day, may, perhaps, furnish a narrative not altogether uninteresting, and not inconsistent with our present purpose. For a western settlement, Chicago can claim no inconsiderable degree of antiquity. In regard to its earlier history, however, very little can be affirmed with any degree of certainty. The original proprietors and first inhabitants of the region were, of course, the aborigines. The description of the first appearance of the vicinity, by some of its earliest explorers, leads to the belief that they were here from a very early period; that this was then, and from time immemorial had been, the site of an Indian village. Maj. Long, among others, mentions the number and apparent antiquity of the trails centreing here as evidence of the truth of this position. It is to be regretted that so little can be ascertained with certainty of the lives and fortunes of the various tribes which, at different times, flourished on the spot. The melancholy truth that they have passed away from their ancient dwelling-places constitutes about all we know of them. Those wild races of primitive men have been swept away by the onward march of civilization. Their rude wigwams and bark canoes have given place to the princely dwellings and the stately ships of another and a different class of beings. Chieftain and warrior are gone. It is only occasionally that a miserable remnant find their way back from their new homes in the more distant west to witness the transformation which is going on in this land of their forefathers. Their visits are becoming less and less frequent. Each year witnesses so many changes that soon they will cease to recognize in the scene any semblance of its former self. All will soon be changed—save only the beating of the waves on the shore of the lake, over which man can exercise no control. The Illinois, the Shawnees, and the Pottawatomies will be no more. They may survive for a time beyond the father of waters, or on the shores of the Pacific, but fate seems to have decreed that, ultimately, the whole race are to become extinct.

The French were the original discoverers and settlers of the west. As early as the latter part of the sixteenth century, while the English Colonies were yet clinging to the shores of the Atlantic, almost two hundred years ago, their voyages and expeditions to this region commenced. In a few years they discovered, and, to some extent, settled, the whole vast region from Canada to the Gulf of Mexico—a distance of more than 3000 miles. Their undertaking, at that early day, was one of no little difficulty and danger. It was, nevertheless, commenced with a spirit, and carried on with a degree of perseverance and sagacity, unexampled in the history of adventure. The limits of the present sketch will not permit us to give the details of these expeditions. It would be unpardonable, however, to pass over in silence the exploits of those brave and self-devoted men, through whose exertions the resources and capabilities of the west were first made known. It is to be feared that they have failed to receive, at the hands of posterity, the reward to which their achievements entitle them; that, while we have been lavish of praise upon the discoverers of other portions of our country, we have failed to pay suitable tribute to the memory of these first pioneers in the region we inhabit—these pilgrim fathers of the west. If to penetrate thousands of miles into the heart of a continent, bidding adieu for months to the comforts of home, braving hunger and thirst and the savage, can be said to command our admiration and gratitude, then these men have distinguished claims upon us who are now reaping the fruits of all their toils and sufferings. The earliest of these expeditions, as well as the most distinguished, were those of Marquette and LaSalle. The former occurred in the year 1673, and resulted in the discovery of the Mississippi—the original object and design of the expedition. To this expedition is probably to be ascribed the honor of paying the first visit to Chicago, it being the prevailing opinion that it passed through here on its return to Canada, ascending the Illinois River and crossing to Michigan. Perrot, by some writers, is believed to have been here a few years earlier. The story of Marquette, who voluntarily remained among the Illinois Indians, and found at last a solitary grave on the eastern shore of Michigan, at the mouth of a river bearing his name, is familiar to all.

With the expedition of LaSalle, in 1680, Chicago cannot be so clearly identified. This expedition, however, was productive of more important consequences to the west, generally, than the preceding one. The Mississippi was navigated to its mouth; forts, at favorable points, erected;

the shores of the great Lakes thoroughly explored, and permanent settlements, at several points, commenced.   The expeditions which succeeded
those of Marquette and LaSalle were of minor importance, being principally designed to sustain the colonies already planted, and to prosecute
the traffic which had previously been entered into with the natives.
Although no positive testimony exists on the subject, it is highly probable
that Chicago was frequently visited by the French during their passages
to and from the west.   Having once been here, they must ever after
have appreciated the advantages of the situation, both in a commercial
and military point of view,—their sagacity in these matters seldom failed
them.   In their magnificent scheme of a chain of military posts, connecting
Canada and the Gulf of Mexico, Chicago, doubtless, formed an important
link, being at the head of the Lakes, and affording so many facilities to
attain the interior.

The French Colonies in the west, sustained by emigration, continued
from the first to prosper and flourish.   Under the general name of Louisiana, which they assumed at a later period, they were made the frequent
subject of grants from the crown to individuals and companies.   About
1717, they are found the property of the celebrated Mississippi Company,
which, at the time, gave rise to much speculation throughout Europe.
At the close of the French and Indian War, Louisiana was transferred,
by treaty, to the British.   During the Revolution, the territory comprising
the present State of Illinois became, by conquest, the property of Virginia,
by which State it was erected into a county, under the name of the County
of Illinois.

Virginia ceded it to the General Government at the time of the cession
of western lands by the eastern states.   In 1800, the present State of
Illinois became a part of Indiana Territory, having a population of about
3000.   In 1809, it became a Territory by itself, with a population of
12,282, and, in 1818, was admitted into the Union.

On the 3d of August, 1795, at the treaty held by General Wayne, with
the Pottawatomies and other tribes at Greenville, the title to six miles
square of territory, at the mouth of Chikajo River, as it is expressed in the
treaty, was obtained by the United States.   From the language of this
treaty, it appears that a fort had formerly stood on the land thus ceded,
which renders it pretty certain, that the French, who alone could have
required anything of the sort, had made a settlement here, many years
before.   In 1804, Fort Chicago was built on the site of the present Fort.
About the same time, the American Fur Company, having been organized
shortly before, established a trading station, under the protection of the
Garrison.   The little colony thus planted here, some forty years ago, for
military and trading purposes, may be regarded as the first attempt to
effect a permanent settlement of Chicago.   The regular and monotonous
life led by this little community, for the first eight years, afforded few
incidents worthy of particular notice.   In 1812, however, the war broke
out with England, the consequences of which were peculiarly disastrous to
all the Western settlements, exposed as they were, especially those in
Illinois, to the hostility of neighboring tribes of Indians.   The causes
which conspired to render the Indians hostile at this time, are generally
well understood, and may be traced to the machinations of Tecumseh,
and other English emissaries, whose influence extended through all the
tribes, being felt as far as the remote regions of Lake Superior.   Chicago
being then an extreme frontier post in this direction, and the country in
every direction around it, full of Indians, with a force inadequate to its
defence, was considered so much endangered as to require its evacuation.

This being resolved upon at Detroit, Capt. J. Heald, the officer in command here at the time, received an order 'to abandon the Fort, and proceed with the troops to Fort Wayne. This evacuation, on account of the fatal consequences which followed it, and the fact, that some of our present citizens were themselves here, and had friends here at the time, has always been regarded with interest, and may be considered a memorable event in the annals of Chicago. The transaction may, therefore, not inappropriately be given somewhat in detail, in this connection. Beside the Garrison, there were several families residing here at the time. Mr. John Kinzie, father of John H. Kinzie, Esq., present Register of the Land Office in this City, occupied a house on the North side of the River, a little East of the present site of the Lake House.* The evacuation took place on the 15th of August, six days after the reception of the order from Gen. Hull, and the day before the disgraceful surrender of Detroit, by that officer, and not after, as some writers have erroneously represented it. In the meantime, a larger body of Indians, mostly of the Pottawatomie nation, had assembled in the vicinity of the Fort. This has generally been represented as a voluntary movement on the part of the Indians —but the most correct opinion appears to be, that Capt. Heald collected them himself, requiring of them an escort for the troops, and promising to give them the factory stores, a considerable quantity of which, were on hand at the time. Whether this be the fact, or not, some understanding of the kind undoubtedly existed on the part of the Indians, and the non-fulfillment of the agreement, by Capt. Heald, according to their expectations, may have occasioned the line of conduct which they subsequently adopted, which proved fatal to the lives of 55 of the party, and had well-nigh brought about the destruction of the whole. The stores on hand were composed in part of a quantity of liquor, and some arms and amunition. These it was deemed imprudent to give the Indians—and they were destroyed, a part being thrown into the River, and the residue deposited in a well within the Fort. One of the arms thus disposed of, a brass piece, was found a few years since, by some people employed in dredging the River—another, it is said, remains there to this day. The stores not destroyed were distributed to the Indians. Under these circumstances, about nine o'clock, on the morning of the 15th of August, the party, composed of 54 regulars, 12 militia, and several families, amounting in all to about 70 persons, left the Fort, under the escort of Capt. Wells, and about 30 Miami Indians. Their route lay along the beach of the Lake, between the water on the left, and a succession of sand-hills on the right. They had proceeded about a mile and a half from the Fort, and had attained a point a short distance beyond the present residence of Mr. H. B. Clarke,† and were advancing, unconscious of danger, when Capt. Wells, who it appears, had strayed for some purpose, some distance from the main body, discovered the Indians in ambush behind the sand-hills. At the same time, another party was seen interposing in the rear, between them and the Fort, which they had just left. The alarm was immediately given—the dead march struck up, and the troops marched directly up the bank, upon the Indians. The action did not commence, as has generally been represented, by firing, on the part of the Indians. After firing one round, the troops charged, and succeeded in dispersing the Indians in front. But the disparity of numbers was too great. The most determined bravery was displayed by the troops, but it could avail little against the superior force opposed to them, protected by the sand-hills

* East side of Rush Street, from North Water to Michigan Streets.
† South of Sixteenth Street.

behind which it had entrenched itself. In 15 minutes, nearly the whole
party were killed or wounded, and all the baggage in the possession of
the enemy. Capt. Heald drew off his men, into the open prairie, and
took possession of a slight elevation, out of reach of the bank, and every
other cover. The Indians, after some consultation, made signs for Capt.
Heald to approach them. He was met by a Pottawatomie Chief, called
Blackbird, who requested him to surrender, promising to spare the lives
of the whole party, in case of compliance. After some parley, the terms
were agreed to, and the arms delivered up. The survivors were marched
back to the Indian encampment, near the Fort, about the spot where
State Street now opens to the River, and where the present Market is
located. Here, some of the prisoners, those who had been wounded,
were murdered in the most shocking manner, by the squaws, who appeared to take great delight in exercising their knives and besmearing
them in the blood of their unfortunate victims. The small number sur-
viving, were distributed, according to the custom of the savages, among
the different members of the tribe. Mr. J. Kinzie, Sen., however, whose
family, from the first, had been protected by some friendly chiefs,
although he was himself engaged in the action, with the troops—succeeded
in procuring the release of Capt. Heald and lady, who were sent by him
to St. Joseph, and thence to Mackinaw, whence they made their escape.
The remainder of the prisoners were retained, but, it is said, were treated
with great kindness, and most of them surrendered to the British, at
Detroit, in the following spring. The day following the action, the
Indians burnt down the Fort, and dispersed. Such are the leading particulars of this unfortunate action, collected, principally, from an eye-wit-
ness of the whole. Capt. Heald has been subjected to much blame, a
portion of which was undoubtedly merited. His management of the
Indians was injudicious throughout, and the destruction of the stores, to
say the least, imprudent. The evacuation, under existing circumstances,
was remonstrated against, by Mr. Kinzie and Capt. Wells, both of whom,
from long intercourse with the Indians, had become familiar with their
character, and were enabled to anticipate and foretell the result which
ensued. Capt. Wells had been bred an Indian warrior, and was a brave
and skilful soldier. He unfortunately fell early in the action, and was
found with his face blackened, after the same manner of the Savages,
when they meet with disappointment.

The Fort was rebuilt in 1817, when it took the name of Fort Dearborn.
It was occupied, except at short intervals, by a Garrison, until 1837, when,
the Indians having generally left the country, it was finally evacuated, and
has never since been re-occupied as a military post. It remains in much
the same condition as in '37, except the pallisades, which were removed,
the past spring, and their place supplied by a handsome fence. It has
since been occupied by officers and agents in charge of the public works,
and their families. Fort Dearborn being almost the only memento of
the past, in the midst of so many creations of the day—the necessity of
any alteration in its appearance is to be regretted.

Until 1832, and even so late as 1833, little or nothing was done towards
making a commencement of the City—it probably not entering into the
imagination of any one, previous to that time, that a town of any importance was to be here at all, at least, not for many years. In 1832, its
appearance and condition was much the same as in 1823, when Major
Long, who visited the place that year, describes it "as presenting no
cheering prospects, and containing but few huts, inhabited by a miserable
race of men, scarcely equal to the Indians, from whom they were descended

—and their log or bark houses as low, filthy, and disgusting, displaying not the least trace of comfort, and as a place of business, affording no inducements to the settler—the whole amount of trade on the Lake, not exceeding the cargoes of five or six schooners, even at the time when the Garrison received its supplies from Mackinaw." This picture, though perhaps too highly colored, presents, in the main, a correct view of Chicago, in 1832. In 1830, there had been a sale of Canal lots, the best bringing only fifty or one hundred dollars, many of which have since become the most valuable in the City. Up to about that time, the present most business, and densely populated part of the City, was fenced, and used by the Garrison, for some purpose of husbandry, or pasturage. So late as '35 or '6, the fires usual on the prairies in the fall, overran the third and fourth wards. There were only some five or six houses, built mostly of logs, and a population of less than one hundred.

One of these houses, formerly the property of the Fur Company, was, until a short time past, occupied by Col. Beaubien. About 80 rods to the south of that, stood a house, once occupied by Colonel Owens, but since washed away by the Lake. A house, known as "Cobweb Castle," on block No. 1, was formerly the abode of Dr. Alexander Wolcott.

The dwelling of Mr. John Kinzie stood east of the Lake House. A log building at the corner of Dearborn and South Water Streets, and the once celebrated tavern of Mr. Mark Beaubien, on the site of the Sauganash, generally known as the eagle, together with a building on block 14, and a cabin, occupied by Robinson, the Indian Chief at Wolf Point, constituted all the buildings, except the Fort, to be found here in 1832. Sometime this year, however, Robert A. Kinzie built a store at Wolf Point, the first frame building in Chicago. In 1834, several brick buildings were erected.

The commerce of the place, up to this period, was equally insignificant. In fact, there was none, unless the traffic of the Fur Company, can be dignified with that name. Vessels occasionally ventured here, but so seldom, that the arrival of a schooner was an event of no little moment, and created a sensation throughout the community. The year 1832, may then be regarded as the period from which to date the commencement of the City. Many causes, the Indian war among them, conspired, about this time, to bring Chicago into general notice. What was called the "Western Fever," had begun to rage generally, throughout the country. —Thousands were flocking from the East, to seek homes in the West. The first premonitions of the speculating mania, had manifested themselves. Eligible sites for towns and cities, were sought out, and eagerly appropriated. The superior advantages of Chicago, in this period of general enquiry, when enterprise was universally aroused, and incited by the hope of sudden wealth, could not long escape public attention.

The attention of Congress had been called to the importance and necessity of a harbor, and an appropriation was confidently relied upon at the next session. Gen. Winfield Scott, who explored the country during the Indian war, took a lively interest in this work, and addressed a letter in relation to it, which was subsequently laid before Congress. The construction of the Illinois and Michigan Canal had also been finally resolved upon by the State legislature. Active measures were being taken to survey the different routes, and to estimate the cost of the various plans prepared. Hence the commencement, and completion of this important work at no distant day, might confidently be relied upon. The resources of the State, too, were beginning to be more generally known, and better appreciated. The most alluring reports of the character of the soil—its productiveness—the facilities for making farms on our prairies—together with the salubrity of the climate, were circulated far and wide. The most strenuous exertions were made, and with the most signal success, to promote emigration. Enterprise, stimulated by interest, and the hope of gain, was aroused, calling forth and concentrating upon this one object, all the resources and capabilities of the age. Capital was enlisted, and credit and unlimited confidence invoked to its aid. Money, owing to excessive bank, and even private issues, was abundant, and loans to any amount were effected with the greatest ease. The west suddenly became the centre of men's thoughts and wishes, and Chicago, as the most important point in the west, the goal to which all directed their aspirations.

Such are some of the prominent causes which may be said, at the period referred to, to have given the first impulse to the city. That it grew and prospered as it did, under their operation, will excite no surprise—the result could not well have been otherwise. Its progress, accordingly, until about 1837, has no parallel—it was rapid in the extreme. Buildings went up as if by magic—stores were opened by the hundred, and speedily filled with merchandise; people of every calling and pursuit in life, laborers, mechanics, and professional men, influenced by a common purpose—the hope of success in their several spheres of action—came together here, and entered at once with a zeal and activity into the schemes of improvement projected. The sale of Canal lots, in 1830, has been already mentioned. In 1833, a great Indian payment was held here, near the present site of the Lake House. In the latter part of this year the work on the harbor was commenced, and, during the same year, the present Light-house was erected, the old one having fallen down. In 1835, the population of the place was said to amount to 5500, a computation which probably included transitory persons, a great many of whom were here at the time. The actual population, however, that year, could not have been much less than 3000. In 1836, another sale of Canal lots took place, which was attended with much excitement, and occasioned a large collection of people from distant quarters. The prices were extravagantly high. In 1836, a branch of the State Bank was located here. On the 4th of July, 1836, the ceremony of breaking the first ground on the Canal took place at Canal Port,* in presence of a large concourse of spectators. During the winter of '36-7 the Act to incorporate the City passed the State Legislature, and, in May succeeding, the first election under the Charter was held, which resulted in the choice of Wm. B. Ogden to the office of Mayor. The growth of commerce, thus far, kept pace with everything else. The community were dependent, during the first few years, entirely upon supplies from abroad; this, together with the great influx of emigration, and the travel which began to set in in this direction, gave employment to a considerable amount of shipping, and steamboats and schooners began to ply regularly between this port and Buffalo.

During this brief but exciting period, the community fortunately found time to devote some attention to things of greater importance than the accumulation of this world's goods. Before or during 1836 as many as six churches had been organized, and suitable buildings provided for their accommodation. These churches, together with such as have since been established, have always received a liberal support, and are now in a flourishing condition. Neither was the subject of education wholly neglected. The school section, which, fortunately, lay contiguous to the city, and was proportionately valuable, was disposed of in 1834, and the avails applied

---

* Now Bridgeport.

to the support of common schools. Means for the diffusion of general intelligence were also provided.

In 1834, John Calhoun commenced the publication of the *Chicago Democrat*, and in the following year, Thos. O. Davis established the *Chicago American*, both of which papers still exist—the latter under the name of the *Chicago Express*, being published daily. These papers, together with the *Prairie Farmer* (Agricultural), the *Western Citizen* (Abolition), the *North-Western Baptist* (Baptist), and the *Better Covenant* (Universalist), which have since been started, are ably conducted, and have an extensive circulation.

The year 1837 is especially memorable in the annals of Chicago as the period of protested notes. It was during this year that the consequences of speculation, (?) which had hitherto operated most favorably for the west, were experienced to a most ruinous extent. Chicago was intimately connected with speculation through all its progress. It was in its incipient stages at the period of the commencement of the city, but a disposition and tendency to it was apparent even then. It raged with great violence during '35-6, and a portion of '37, at which time it gave color and direction to most business transactions.

The history of this singular delusion is replete with instructive incidents. It seems unaccountable to the more sober judgment of these times how men, under any circumstances, could have been led so far astray—how prudence, foresight, and sagacity could, to such an extent, have lost their dominion and control over the human mind. But so it was. The rapid and unprecedented rise in the value of real estate, and the certainty of that rise, exerted a most seductive influence; very few were found able to resist the temptation; all classes of people, ultimately abandoning the usual avocations of society, devoted themselves exclusively to speculation, and hazarded their all upon this sea of chance. This wild spirit found its way ultimately into the halls of legislation, and controlled the conduct and policy of states, as it had done that of individuals. It was under the influence of this spirit that those stupendous schemes of internal improvement originated in many of the new states, which have entailed upon subsequent times the evils of debt, taxation, and, in some cases, national disgrace and dishonor.—Speculation led, in short, to the perpetration, on all hands, of acts of folly and absurdity seldom before heard of. The sources of wealth being regarded as inexhaustible, naturally created extravagant ideas of prosperity, and afforded to all the apparent means of indulging in every species of expenditure. It would be useless to follow speculation through its stages, as one act of absurdity succeeded another in rapid succession.—Are not these times and their consequences written in effaceless characters upon the memory of every reader?

But the day of wrath and retribution was at hand. Confidence and credit, too long abused, refused any longer to lend their aid. The unfortunate victims of the delusion were suddenly awakened from their dream of wealth to the certainty of almost universal bankruptcy and ruin. Thousands, suddenly called upon to investigate the condition of their affairs, which, in the excitement of the moment, no one thought it necessary to attend to, found themselves involved to the extent of thousands and hundreds of thousands of dollars, and their real estate, from which alone the means of payment could come, depreciated in value—in fact, unsaleable at any price. Thousands, from affluence, were reduced, without warning or preparation, to poverty; some struggled for a time with their destiny, but the evil day came at last; and scarcely one, ultimately, survived the catastrophe. The comparatively small number of those who

did finally escape the ordeal, it has been observed were, indebted more to
chance and good luck than to any unusual endowment of prudence and
sagacity.   The ablest business men of the age—those in whose judgment
and capacity in ordinary times we should unhesitatingly repose the most
implicit confidence; ventured as far and hazarded as much as any in this
dangerous game.   •

To Chicago, in an especial degree, was the stroke which was thus
inflicted upon the business interests of the country injurious and calam-
tious.   It was to her a season of mourning and desolation.   Many of her
most business and enterprising citizens were insolvent—all, to a greater or
less extent, embarrassed in their circumstances.   She had gone on hitherto in a state of uninterrupted prosperity—nothing had thus far occurred to
check the progress of improvement.   Could, that state of prosperity have
continued, Chicago would, by this time have ranked among the proudest
cities of the land.   But calamity came suddenly and unexpectedly; and,
for a time, she quailed under its effects.

But she was not, and could not be, entirely prostrated.   Her position
was too favorable, and her redeeming powers too abundant to permit her
very long to be seriously affected by any calamity, however great.   She
had, in common with the west, gained much by speculation.   What had
been accomplished could not be undone.   Her works of improvement
survived—her population was left to her, and more than all, her great and
inexhaustible natural resources remained to bear her on to the consummation of her high destiny.   Her citizens returned to their habits of industry
and economy, from which the force of evil example had seduced them.
Her business men, taught a severe lesson by the past, bent all their energies, and called into requisition all their experience to build up their
injured credit, and to restore their business to a safe and permanent
foundation.   The consequences began gradually to develop themselves.
But little was gained during '38–39; but in '40, things assumed a more
favorable aspect, and since that time the increase of business and population has been most rapid.   This will be more fully illustrated by a reference to the census of different periods, and to the tabular statements of
the amount, value, and character of the export and import trade of the
place during each year, contained in another part of this volume.

It is with feelings of pride and satisfaction that the friends of Chicago
can refer to the experience of the past six years, as furnishing an enduring
monument to the industry, enterprise, and perseverance of her people, and
as establishing, beyond controversy, the existence and permanency of her
sources of prosperity.   If, with an impoverished community, at a period
of general prostration of the business interests of the country, under the
pressure of heavy municipal and enormous State liabilities, with resources
comparatively undeveloped, and the works of public improvement unfinished, Chicago has accomplished so much, what may not reasonably be
expected when these and all obstacles are removed from her way?

A glance at her geographical position will convince the most skeptical
that Chicago is but the nucleus about which is destined to grow up, at no
remote period, one of the most important commercial towns in the west.
Situated on the waters of the only great Lake exclusively within the
United States—being the termination, on the one hand, of the navigation
of the Lakes, and on the other, of the Illinois and Michigan Canal—
affording great natural facilities for a harbor, by means of Chicago River
and its branches—the excelling site for a capacious ship basin in the very
heart of the town, at the junction of said branches—having dependent
upon it a region of country vast in extent, and of extraordinary fertility,

it must always be the dividing point between two great sections of the Union, where the productions of each must meet and pay tribute. It is susceptible of the easiest demonstration that the route by the Lakes, the Canal, and the Western Rivers, when once the channels of communication are completed, will, for cheapness, safety, and expedition, possess advantages superior to every other. Among the advantages of this route, the climate, so favorably adapted to the preservation of produce, deserves especial notice.

The commercial interests, then, of the east, and especially of the great valley of the west, will be intimately connected with Chicago, as a place of transshipment and deposit—and the value and amount of trade in produce, in lumber, salt, and in every description of merchandize which will centre here, is beyond our present powers of computation, and can only be measured by the future wants and capabilities of the country.

Those important works—the harbor and canal—upon which so many interests depend, justly demand the most serious consideration; and it is highly gratifying to allude to their present most flattering prospects. It is now reduced almost to a certainty, that Chicago, after the expenditure of so much solicitude, and a large amount of money, is speedily to be furnished with a safe, commodious, and permanent harbor. Under the supervision of our present able superintendent, the work is prosecuted with a degree of vigor that must be crowned with success.

The principal difficulty encountered during the progress of the harbor has been occasioned by the deposition of sand and the formation of bars at its mouth. The plans heretofore adopted to surmount this difficulty have failed upon trial, and are now abandoned. Two plans have been proposed the present season, which have attracted considerable attention. One of these, suggested by Captain J. McClellan, the present superintendent, recommends the construction of a pier north of the present ones, at a distance from them greater than the length of the present bar, and is based upon the supposition that the sand would form a bar around its head, and not reach the entrance of the harbor. The other plan, which has been adopted, and is now being carried into effect, proposes the extension of the north pier, in the form of a circle, a distance of 990 feet, which will bring it into the line of the original direction of that pier. A good channel for vessels of every class will then exist from the head of the south pier, around the bar, that pier being extended no farther into the Lake. If this plan succeed, Chicago will be furnished with a harbor, not inferior to any on the Lakes.

We have the most flattering assurance that the work upon our other and not less important branch of public improvement—the Illinois and Michigan Canal—will be resumed the coming season, under the operation of the late law of the Legislature. The history of this great work, which was contemplated from the first settlement of the State, and has been the subject of legislation for more than twenty years, presents a remarkable instance of the obstacles which frequently oppose the accomplishment of the greatest undertakings. The first survey of the canal was made in 1823. In 1825, a bill was passed to incorporate the Illinois and Michigan Canal Company; but no stock being taken under the charter, it was repealed at the next special session. In 1827, act of March 2, Congress appropriated each alternate section of land within five miles of the proposed line. In 1829, a board of commissioners was organized, with power to determine upon the route, and to discharge other duties connected with the work. Chicago, Ottawa, and other towns on the line, were laid out by the board, and sales of lots effected. The work was commenced in the year 1836, and was suspended in 1842. The law under which this work was contracted, provides that the canal shall be 60 feet wide at the surface, 40 feet at the base, and six feet deep; that it shall commence at Chicago, on canal land, and terminate at the mouth of the Little Vermillion River, making a distance of 95½ miles. It was to be constructed upon the deep cut principle, and to be fed from the waters of Lake Michigan. By a recent survey, a method has been discovered by which it is believed that a sufficient supply of water can be procured from Fox River for a canal upon the shallow cut plan. The sum of about $5,-000,000 has thus far been expended upon the work. To complete it upon the plan contemplated by the late law, about $1,600,000 more has been estimated to be necessary. If that law goes into effect, as present appearances seem clearly to indicate, the canal will be finished in about three years. We shall then have the greatest continuity of inland water communication in the world—extending from the Atlantic Ocean by the Erie Canal, along the chain of Lakes, through our canal, the Illinois and Mississippi Rivers, to the Gulf of Mexico. This will be a glorious consummation for Illinois, and for every interest connected with her. The vast resources connected with the canal itself, the resources which it will develope throughout the State, will enable her in a short time to discharge all her debts—to establish her credit—and to redeem her reputation. Already has the prospect of the completion of this work effected a revolution in public sentiment, and has caused emigration to set strongly in this direction. The reports which have been circulated in regard to the circumstances and prospects of the State have been discovered, upon examination, to be founded in falsehood and misrepresentation. The public are now satisfied that the climate is as healthy and salubrious as any portion of the west—that the soil is infinitely superior—that our taxes, even under the effect of that severe ordeal through which we have passed, uniformly have been less than any of the adjoining States and Territories—and that the prospects of the value of real estate, the high price of produce, and the facilities of a convenient market, will render it the most desirable State in the Union. We may trust that the day is not far distant when Illinois will assume her proper position among the States of the Union—when her friends will be enabled to hurl back the imputations which have been cast upon her character—when she can no longer, with a shadow of truth or justice, be stigmatized as the land of speculators and repudiation! Until then, she must calmly bide her time.

In conclusion of our subject, it may be proper to refer more particularly to some important considerations and facts connected with the present condition of Chicago, hitherto only incidentally alluded to.

The city, for some time past, has been considerably embarrassed with debt, in consequence of the necessity which has existed of borrowing money to carry on its works of improvement. The existing liabilities of the city amount to $8977.55, viz.: bonds to Strachan & Scott, $5000; bonds for Clark Street Bridge, $3000; bonds for barrier to the Lake, and interest, $977.55. The increasing revenues derived from taxation and other sources will soon afford the means to extinguish these liabilities entirely. The tax of the present year, at the rate of assessment of this year, amounts to $7852.45; the school tax, at half a mill per cent., to $685.24. A large amount of city property, which heretofore has been unproductive, will, the next year, become taxable, particularly the Canal lands and the reservation. The amount of the tax for the coming year, unless a reduction should take place, may safely be estimated at $12,000. In addition to this, there is now in the treasury, unappropriated, $1854, and the current expenses paid. The management of the fiscal affairs of the city, by our present common council, is entitled to the highest praise. The financial ability of the mayor has been recently tested in the management of a negotiation at New York, by which a reduction of three per cent. has been effected upon the interest of the largest debt of the city, and may be regarded as equivalent to a new loan. The credit of the city is now established upon a permanent foundation, and cannot be easily shaken. City scrip for some time has been at par.

Our common schools are worthy of especial notice. They are sustained in part by the school fund, and in part by taxation. The fund originally amounted to about $39,000; but nearly one-half of this amount has been lost by injudicious loans. These schools are justly the pride of the city, and the interest which is manifested in them is an evidence of the importance which the community attaches to education. We have also a medical college chartered by the Legislature in 1837, and several schools sustained by private munificence. Independent of these, we have several other institutions, which are exerting a beneficial influence. Among them, the Mechancis' Institute and the Young Men's Association are prominent in importance. These institutions, while sustained as they have been hitherto, will be both useful and ornamental to the city. Both of them have libraries, containing, in the aggregate, about 2500 volumes. The Mechanics' Institute has a department in the *Prairie Farmer*, devoted exclusively to the interests of the mechanical arts, — the Young Mens' Association a reading room, where most of the publications of the day are regularly received, and accessible to the public. There is, in addition to these libraries, a circulating library, containing about 1500 volumes. We have other societies designed to meet the intellectual wants of the community, among which may be mentioned the Chicago Lyceum—the oldest literary society in the place. Our theatre—a very pretty one—has been in operation the past season, and met with some encouragement; but it must be confessed that, at present, the prospects of the drama are not flattering.

The book making and publishing business has been commenced under favorable auspices. In illustration of the condition of this department of trade, we may allude to the third volume of Mr. SCAMMON'S REPORTS OF THE SUPREME COURT, printed by Messrs. ELLIS & FERGUS, and now about ready for publication. The fact that the execution of this volume is equal, if not superior to the two former ones, which were issued from two of the best presses of the East, is highly creditable to our city, and must be gratifying to the profession generally.

In facilities for the accommodation of the travelling public, Chicago has made great progress. In early times our inns were miserable in the extreme. Now we have eighteen hotels and houses of public entertainment, some of them large and splendid establishments, not inferior to any in the West. The great amount of travel passing through here during the season of navigation renders tavern keeping a very profitable branch of business.

An extensive staging business has grown up here, and may be referred to as an instance of enterprise and public spirit on the part of those engaged in it. The several lines of stages centring here, for speed, safety, and comfort, are not excelled by any in the country.

The Hydraulic Company, designed to supply the city with pure water from the Lake, was incorporated in 1836, and has already been the source of great utility to the city, both in supplying water for domestic purposes, and for the extinguishment of fires. The stock is owned principally by merchants, and in time must become the source of great profit.

Ship building has been carried on here to some extent. A steam propeller, registering 270 tons, was built the past season, and a schooner of about 200 tons burthen, to be called the Maria, is now in process of construction by the same builder, and will probably be launched in the spring.

It will be seen by reference to the statistical tables of this year, that a large amount of beef has been packed here the present season. We have four large packing-houses, and all of them have done a heavy business thus far. The pork-packing is only just commencing, but will, it is thought, be extensive.

Much might be said in commendation of our Fire Companies—all of which are highly efficient, and bespeak the public spirit of our citizens. Our Military Companies will speak for themselves.

Considering the age of the city, and the fact that our population has been derived from almost every nation under heaven, and speak so many different languages—the existing state of its society confers distinction upon Chicago. Among the new cities of the west, we shall be entitled, in this particular, at the present time, to an enviable position; the means now adopted to improve the condition of society will, at no distant day, enable us to rank with any city in the land. Our citizens have always been distinguished for intelligence and morality—and for the uniform observance of all the proprieties of life. Our common schools, as the means of educating the rising generation, have always been regarded with the deepest interest, have been abundantly provided with the means of their support, and are conducted with great ability. The most scrupulous care is exercised, on the part of the inspectors of public instruction, in the selection of teachers; the schools are subjected to frequent examination—and their exists much emulation among the teachers.

The most becoming respect is paid to the institutions and forms of public worship. Our numerous churches and religious societies enable everyone to worship God according to the dictates of conscience. Whatever opinions may be entertained in regard to religion, it will be acknowledged that a decent respect for its ordinances is greatly promotive of the well-being and prosperity of any community.

The peace and good order of society is worthy of remark.—Brawls and affrays are extremely rare in our streets—and it may justly be said, that a more peaceable and quiet population can no where be found.

It will be impossible in this connection to mention particularly all the institutions which testify the public spirit and benevolence of the community. Reference, however, can be had to subsequent parts of the book, where they are more particularly described.

We have now followed our subject to its conclusion. We have attempted to exhibit Chicago as it was in gone-by days—to mark the successive stages of its progress—and to delineate its condition at the present time.

We have reason to be proud of our city—not so much on account of its relative size among the other cities of the land—of its present population—and the amount and value of its commerce—but as affording a sublime illustration of what man, under circumstances of great difficulty and embarrassment, can accomplish in a short space of time.

In the hope that its future history may be worthy of the past—that the experience of the next and each succeeding year may justify our favorable predictions of it in regard to its high destiny—we must, for the present, bid adieu to the QUEEN CITY OF THE NORTH-WEST.

PORT OF CHICAGO.

CAPT. SETH JOHNSTON, DEPUTY COLLECTOR AND INSPECTOR.

Revenue Office, 38 Clark Street.

The following tabular statements will exhibit, with an approach to accuracy, the amount and value of the trade of Chicago, to the close of the present year, 1843. A very serious difficulty has existed, heretofore, in ascertaining the actual amount of exports and imports of the place, especially the exports, owing to the fact, that a great many vessels arrive and depart, during the season of navigation, without being reported at the Custom House, or leaving any evidence of the character and amount of their cargoes. The existence of this difficulty was more particularly set forth in a memorial of the Common Council to Congress, in the year 1840, in which they allow a deduction of one-third from the amount known, to be added, for the amount unknown. It has been thought advisable, in the following statement, to give only the actual amount, as ascertained from record in the revenue office, it being understood, from the above explanation, that the estimate is considerably below the true amount:

EXPORTS.		IMPORTS.	
1836	$1,000.64	1836	$325,203.90
1837	11,065.00	1837	373,667.12
1838	16,044.75	1838	579,174.61
1839	33,843.00	1839	630,980.26
1840	228,635.74	1840	562,106.20
1841	348,362.24	1841	564,347.88
1842	659,305.20	1842	664,347.88

ARTICLES EXPORTED DURING THE YEAR 1842.

Wheat,	586,907 bushels.	Flour,	2,920 bbls.
Corn,	35,358 "	Beef,	762 "
Oats,	53,486 "	Pork and Hams,	15,447 "
Peas,	484 "	Fish,	915 "
Barley,	1,090 "	Lard,	367,200 lbs.
Flax Seed,	750 "	Tallow,	151,300 "
Hides, No. of	6,947	Soap,	2,400 "
Brooms, No. of	5,587	Candles,	500 "
Maple Sugar,	4,500 lbs.	Tobacco,	3,000 "
Lead,	59,990 "	Butter,	24,200 "
Feathers,	2,409 "	Wool,	1,500 "
Furs and Peltries,	446 Packs.		

ARTICLES EXPORTED DURING THE YEAR 1843.

Wheat	628,967 bushels.	Tobacco	74,900 pounds.
Corn	2,443 "	Lead	360,000 "
Oats	3,767 "	Wool	22,050 "
Flax seed	1,920 "	Candles	4,900 "
Pork	11,112 barrels.	Soap	5,300 "
Lard	2,823 "	Packages Furs	393 "
Beef	10,380 "	Brooms	180 dozen
Tallow	1,133 "	Flour	10,786 barrels.
Hides	14,536		

ARTICLES IMPORTED DURING THE YEAR 1843.

Merchandise	2,012 tons	Shingles	4,117,025
" "	101,470 pkgs.	Square timber	16,600 feet
Salt	27,038 barrels	Staves,	57,000
Whiskey	2,585 "	Bark	430 cords
Lumber	7,545,142 feet		

Vessels arrived and cleared during the years 1842–3:

	Arrived.	Cleared.	Total.	Aggregate Tons.
1842.	705	705	1410	117,711
1843.	756	691	1447	289,852

A number of vessels left port this year, without being reported.

During the present season, 14,856 barrels of beef have been packed at the several packing houses in the City; only a small portion of this has been exported. The quantity of hides and tallow is not known, but will bear a proportion to the quantity of beef. An amount of pork will be put up here the coming winter, greatly exceeding any former season. No statement in regard to this department, can be made in this connection, as the business is but just commencing.

POPULATION, AUGUST 1, 1843.

MALES:	Ward, 1st.	2d.	3d.	4th.	5th.	6th.	Totals.	
10 yrs and under,	245	284	57	65	100	257	1008	
Over 10 and under 21,	146	133	41	36	63	143	562	
Over 21 and under 45,	627	614	130	102	155	439	2067	
Over 45 and under 60,	25	39	7	8	9	40	128	
Over 60,	5	8	2	2	0	10	27	3792
FEMALES:								
10 yrs and under,	217	271	87	64	98	280	1017	
Over 10 and under 21,	186	183	31	27	37	166	630	
Over 21 and under 45,	398	384	94	73	106	338	1393	
Over 45 and under 60,	27	29	7	6	11	36	116	
Over 60,	7	7	1	1	2	16	34	3190
Colored males under 21,	2	6	0	0	0	4	12	
Colored males over 21,	9	14	2	2	0	3	30	
Colored females under 21,	3	4	0	0	0	3	10	
Colored females over 21,	2	9	0	0	0	2	13	65
Transient persons,	87	246	50	28	19	103	533	533
Population 1843,	1986	2231	509	414	600	1840	7580	7580
Population 1840,	1197	1467	251	179	436	1323	4853	
Increase,	789	764	258	235	164	517	2727	

Whole number of Families, 1177.

Number of Irish,	170	206	29	50	175	143	773	
Germans & Norwegians,	104	217	32	21	90	352	816	
Natives other countries,	134	156	80	84	50	163	667	
Americans,	1578	1652	368	259	285	1182	5324	7580,

(From the Chicago Inter-Ocean.)
THE ANNALS OF CHICAGO.

A lecture delivered before the Chicago Lyceum, Jan. 21, 1840,
by JOSEPH N. BALESTIER. Republished from the original
edition of 1840, with an introduction written by the author
in 1876, and also a review of the lecture published in the
Chicago *Tribune* in 1872. Chicago: Fergus Printing Company.

The lecture here reprinted met with much favor in its day,
and has since received the honor of being advertised for by
the British Museum. The author, now a hale old gentleman,
living in Vermont, writes an exceedingly witty and interesting
introduction, and the entire *brochure* will prove a veritable
treasure to the true lover of Chicago, its ancient history, and
its wonderful progress and possibilities. The entire story reads
like some tale of Arabian enchantment, but truth is strange—
stranger than fiction—and while the Chicagoan of 1840 crossed
at Clark street in a scow ferry-boat, and the city boasted its
4479 inhabitants, the citizen of to-day parades the finest streets
upon the continent, and forms but a small atom among the
525,000 human beings who swarm within our gates. Mr.
Balestier estimates the population to be in 1911 at 2,000,000,
and we must admit that his logic is founded upon very solid
premises. He notes an interesting fact, that the editors in
those days wrote sharp—not to say abusive—squibs against each
other; and makes the following remark, which must be taken,
we fear, with a considerable number of grains of common
salt: "Among the moral prodigies of the past thirty-five years
is the total disappearance of all scurrility and injustice from
the newspapers. This is notably the case in Chicago, where
all is courtesy and respect between editors; where everything is
fair in politics; and the scriptural question, 'Art thou in health,
my brother?' is always scripturally put." The lecture is an
excellent historical condensation, and is not only well written,
but exceedingly readable. It seems a little surprising that its
author, who, upon his own showing, is only 61 years of age, has
not been invited to come and repeat his lecture in the heart of
the city whose greatness he predicted thirty-six years ago.

☞ The "ANNALS OF CHICAGO," a lecture delivered by
Joseph N. Balestier, Esq., issued in neat pamphlet form by
Fergus Printing Company, of this city, comes to our table. It
is a very valuable document, relating to the early and continued
history of this, the liveliest city in the world. It should be in
every library in the State.—*Pomeroy's Democrat.*

(From the Chicago Tribune.)

THE ANNALS OF CHICAGO.

Such is the title of a lecture before the Chicago Lyceum, Jan. 21, 1840, by J. N. Balestier; with an introduction by the author, written in 1876; and also a review of the lecture by a correspondent of THE CHICAGO TRIBUNE; just republished by the Fergus Printing Company, of this city. The lecture has been out of print for several years; but a correspondent of the TRIBUNE found a copy in the State Library at Madison, Wis., and Mr. R. Fergus has done an excellent service to the city by having a copy made, and republishing it. Probably not one in a thousand of our present citizens knew that such a lecture was ever delivered. It was well and ably done; and, as it is the oldest thing of the kind extant, and its contents are comprehensive and valuable, we hope it will be so widely distributed in our private and public libraries that there will be no danger of all the copies being destroyed in any fire that may hereafter occur in the history of the city.

The first number of "The Annals of Chicago" has been received from the Fergus Printing Company, who are to be credited with issuing a very handsome piece of typography. This first number of the "Annals" covers a lecture delivered in 1840, by Joseph N. Balestier, on the early history of the city. The lecture, with introduction and notes, makes a cheerful pamphlet of forty-eight pages, covering much valuable and hitherto inaccessible information. The same publishers propose soon to issue a complete "Directory of the City of Chicago" in 1839.—*The Chicago Tribune.*

CHICAGO, *January 15, 1876.*

ROBERT FERGUS, ESQ.,

Dear Sir:—I am greatly indebted to you for your kind consideration in sending me "The Annals of Chicago," with Introduction, etc., by Mr. Balestier; and Notes. You have done a good work in this republication. I knew Mr. B. very well, although I did not hear the lecture. At that time I was residing on my farm in Will County, having been driven there by failing health, in 1839, after a residence of six years in Chicago.

To the first settlers of Chicago everything relating to its early history possesses peculiar interest, and so to them at least your pamphlet is a treasure.   Yours very truly,

J. D. CATON.

LETTERS OF APPROVAL.

CHICAGO, *Feb. 23, 1876.*

ROBERT FERGUS, ESQ.: *My dear Sir:*—I have looked over with great interest the copy of the "Chicago Directory, 1839," which you have kindly handed me, and sincerely thank you for the pleasure the perusal has afforded me. I am surprised to find how many of the persons whose names you give were personally known to me, and still more surprised to find that, thus far, I have not recalled to recollection the name of a person whom I did know that is omitted. I trust you may find encouragement to go on in your enterprise, and reproduce, as far as possible, these early publications, so important in establishing the early history of the Town.

Yours, very truly,

MARK SKINNER.

CHICAGO, ILL., *February 21, 1876.*

ROBERT FERGUS: *Dear Sir:*—I have carefully read every word in your "Chicago Directory of 1839," and I hasten to thank you for the very great industry by which it is characterized, and to express my great pleasure at its correctness. I was personally acquainted, at that time, with almost every man in the city, and my memory has not yet begun to fail. Besides, I have succeeded in collecting many copies, and parts of copies, of my old Chicago Democrat. And I know what I say when I say you have done your work well.

Yours of olden time,

JOHN WENTWORTH.

CHICAGO, *February 23d, 1876.*

ROB'T FERGUS, ESQ.: *Dear Sir,*—I have carefully examined your "Chicago Directory for 1839," and am pleased to say that it will compare favorably, for correctness, with any Directory published since. I was, at that time, and for several years previous had been, acquainted with nearly all the residents of the city, and do not recollect the name of any person who has been omitted. Yours Truly,

JAMES H. REES.

LETTERS OF APPROVAL.

CHICAGO, *February 22d, 1876.*

MR. ROBERT FERGUS: *Dear Sir,*—I have, with great interest, carefully examined the proof sheets of your re-publication of the "Chicago Directory of 1839" (with which you *then* had much to do), as revised and corrected by yourself and many others, still here, who were then active in embryo Chicago. There are but few corrections that I could suggest, and, on the whole, since the destruction of historical material in the Great Fire of 1871, your publication will, in my opinion, be invaluable as a basis for the history of Chicago. You deserve well of the public, and I trust you may be well repaid for the great labor this publication must have caused you.

Respectfully Yours,

JULIAN S. RUMSEY.

CHICAGO, *February 25th, 1876.*

ROBERT FERGUS: *Dear Sir:*—I have looked over your "Chicago Directory for 1839," with much care, and it gives me pleasure to say that, so far as my recollection serves me, it is quite accurate, and contains the names of all the persons who were then residents of this place. The Directory furnishes much useful information. I hope you may be compensated for your care, labor, and trouble.

Yours, etc.,   E. PECK.

CHICAGO, *February 28th, 1876.*

ROBERT FERGUS, ESQ.: *Dear Sir:*—Allow me to thank you for the pleasure I have derived from a perusal of your very interesting and valuable compilation, "The Chicago Directory of 1839"—the proof-sheets of which you were kind enough to send me. I have examined the work very attentively, and with a view to supply, if needful, any omissions or inaccuracies, but I am pleased to have to say that the thoroughness with which you have done your work leaves me really nothing to suggest.

As you, doubtless, well know, there were few residents of our city in those early days (I question if there was one) that was not personally known to me, and my memory is still green as to all that pertains to that period; when I assure you, therefore, that I have failed to discover a single error either in names, events, or localities, you may safely assume (pardon my seeming presumption in saying so) that there are none.

Your publication will prove a valuable contribution to the literature of early Chicago, and a great help to the future historian. It has afforded me unmixed delight to be thus able to verify my own reminiscences, and I am sure the public will heartily appreciate the service you have rendered them.

I remain, yours, for "auld lang syne,"

MAHLON D. OGDEN.

BIOGRAPHICAL SKETCHES

of

Some *of the* **Early Settlers** *of the*

City of Chicago

William H. Brown
Benjamin W. Raymond
J. Young Scammon
Charles Walker
Thomas Church

HERITAGE BOOKS
2019

I am Yours truly
W. H. Brown

Number Six

Short Biographical Sketches
of Some of Chicago's Early Settlers

Part 2:

Hon. William H. Brown, Benjamin W. Raymond, Esq.,
Hon. J. Young Scammon, Charles Walker, Esq.,
and Thomas Church, Esq.

HON. WILLIAM H. BROWN.

[From the Chicago Magazine, March, 1857.]

To write a sketch of some living men which would be truthful and at the same time readable, which shall present their virtues in due relation to their faults, and as relieved by them, without injustice to the feelings of the parties concerned, is not an easy matter.

Some men are, like the head of a certain statesman, of which the phrenologist could make nothing, because he could find no "bump" about it—it was symmetrically smooth in every part—while others exhibit such decided traits of character, that inequalities are a matter of necessity. Their virtues and their failings alike exhibit themselves decidedly, and in natural correspondence with each other.

Mr. Brown, the subject of this sketch, is a man of marked and decided traits. What he knows, he knows; what he says, he means; and whatever subject comes before him elicits, without delay, a plump and square opinion. Such men must of necessity cross somebody's track, in the course of their lives, and will come to be somewhat differently regarded by different classes of people.

While, therefore, this sketch will endeavor to set forth Mr. Brown as he is, as far as it goes, it cannot of course enter upon such a discussion as would be called for were he not yet moving among us.

Mr. Brown is a native of the State of Connecticut, and was born about the beginning of the nineteenth century. His father was a native of Rhode Island; his profession was that of the law, which he practiced for some twenty-five years, at Auburn, N.Y., with decided talent and success, and then removed to the City of New York, where, a few years since, he died.

The son William, gained his education, as many young men of his time were accustomed to do, while the country was not as well supplied with schools of a high grade as at present, partly in the office of his father, and at various schools; but not extending it in youth, far beyond what are considered good business acquirements. He studied law with his father, and then engaged in its practice with him.

In December, 1818, about the time of his majority, as we infer, he came to seek his fortune in the farther or extreme West, as it then was; and opened a law office in the old French town of Kaskaskia, in this State. His inducement to select Illinois as the State of his residence, he declared to be, that it had, in the summer of that year, adopted a *free* Constitution; without which he would by no means have taken a residence in it. In the spring of 1819, he was appointed a Clerk of the United States Court, which office he held for the period of sixteen years. The seat of government being removed to Vandalia, and the law requiring the Clerk of the Court to keep his office at the Capitol of the State, Mr. Brown followed it thither in December, 1820. He immediately purchased one-half the proprietary interest in a newspaper then published, and called "*The Illinois Intelligencer.*" This paper dated back to 1815, and was the first newspaper ever established in the Territory. Mr. Brown entered upon its editorial duties, and continued in that connection until February, 1823. His partner in the paper was Mr. Wm. Berry, who was a member of the legislature of 1823; which legislature passed a resolution for a convention to alter the Constitution of the State, with a view to the introduction of slavery. The means, by which this resolution went through the legislature, were of a very high-handed character, which the reader will find somewhat illustrated on pages 52-3 of Ford's History of Illinois; and in a lecture delivered before the Historical Society of Chicago, by Mr. Brown.

Mr. Berry voted for this resolution, while Mr. Brown the editor was against it, and denounced it in such terms as he thought applicable to the case. Having prepared an article for the next paper, which exposed the scandalous measures by which the resolution had been carried through the House of Representatives, and having taken proofs of it, preparatory to its insertion, these proofs were surreptitiously taken from the office; and being read by the parties implicated, a storm was at once raised, such as is not uncommon, even in our day, when this same question of slavery is at stake. The usual remedy for such impertinent boldness was at once proposed, *viz.:* a mob, which should demolish the office, and send Mr. Brown about other business. Luckily, Mr. Brown had friends, and his friends had pluck; and their rally saved the office. The paper containing the awful exposition appeared; and was deemed such an indignity to the august body whose doings had been censured, that a resolution was adopted citing the author to their bar. To this citation Mr. Brown declined to answer; giving as his reason, that the Constitution secured the liberty of the Press: and so the resolution went over as unfinished business, and the wounded honor of the House was committed to the tender mercies of the time for its healing.

The partnership in the Illinois Intelligencer came to an end, by the sale of Mr. Brown's interest; and the paper advocated the convention—or in other words, the introduction of slavery

—for the next year. By some reasons, nevertheless, not made public, the paper was given into other editorial hands, some eight months before the vote was taken, and, during that time, did good service in the canvass for freedom.

As Mr. Brown had embarked in the cause of freedom in the State, and had determined to leave it, should the folly of re-introducing slavery prevail, he now gave most of his time to writing and working against that policy; and did much toward securing the verdict rendered in the 2000 majority which forbid its establishment; for which we who now dwell here, and our posterity, will owe him a debt of gratitude and honor.

In December, 1822, the subject of this sketch was married to Miss Harriet C. Seward, daughter of Col. John Seward, deceased, then of Montgomery Co., Ill. Mrs. Brown is the mother of four living sons and one daughter; of whom three are now in active business, and two in the course of their education.

Mr. Brown removed with his family to Chicago, in October, 1835, having been appointed cashier of a branch of the State Bank of Illinois, which had been created here in the winter of 1834. This position he had accepted with some reluctance, under the impression that his previous pursuits had not been of a kind to give him that knowledge of financial matters required in the charge of such an institution. In urging upon him the appointment, one of the principal stockholders remarked, that he possessed one qualification very necessary: in that he could say NO, as easily as most men could say YES. As soon as the proper arrangements could be completed, the bank commenced operations, and continued as the only institution of the kind till the year 1843.

The Bank prospered well under Mr. Brown's management, and might, perhaps, have been prospering yet, had the state of the country been anywise settled and healthy. But the serious derangements commencing in 1836, or rather back of that period, in the financial affairs of the nation, carried away bank, and business, East and West; and the Illinois State Bank did not escape. It suffered great losses, and these, with adverse legislation, induced the stockholders to wind it up. The Chicago branch suffered with the rest; for real estate was forced upon it in place of money. Yet, in the aggregate, it was so managed that the profit and loss would have shown a balance on the right side.

At the time of Mr. Brown's arrival in the State, its population was not over 40,000; and none, or next to none, of them lived north of the present limits of Bond County. When he came to Chicago, it was a village of about two years' growth, and con-tained about 2000 people. All Northern Illinois was a wilder-ness; and, two years later, the whole north half of the State was included in one congressional district; and sent Hon. John T. Stuart, of Springfield, to Congress; electing him over his com-

petitor, Stephen A. Douglas, who, on that occasion, made his
first appearance on the stage in pursuit of political honors. The
writer of this sketch cast his first vote in Illinois against Mr.
Douglas, at that time, and made one of the five majority which
defeated him.

In the conduct of such an institution, through times such as
these, there were two things which it were impossible to secure
together. One was the safety of the institution, and the other,
the good-will of all the community. Everybody was in a condition of suffering, and wanted money, with an intensity that
could take no denial; and the very urgency of the want, point-
ed, in no inconsiderable number of cases, to .the very reason
which made it unsafe to accommodate them. The Cashier of
a bank must of necessity look to the safety of his trust. If he
is faithful to that, no matter whether *no* is an easy word to
him or not; he is forced to make the two letters which com-
pose it, current in his institution. *No*, is not a popular word,
with men who wish to borrow money, especially if they wish
to borrow it very much; as those then did, who wanted to
borrow it at all. Mr. Brown's peculiar qualification already
mentioned perhaps conduced more to the safety of his trust,
than to his popularity for the time being. But integrity and
decision vindicate themselves sooner or later, and he has lost
little in the long run. Indeed the men who supposed themselves to suffer from lack of a decision in their favor, would
now often choose him as the very man to take charge of a trust
of their own, had they one, requiring sagacity and decision
united with integrity in its management.

The building, in which the bank was kept, stood at the S. W.
cor. of LaSalle and South Water Sts.; and is well remembered
by all the oldest residents of the city. It has only disappeared
within the last four or five years.

While the bank was in operation, Chicago was confined principally to the vicinity of the river. The dwellings even, did
not stretch far away from the centre. In the spring of 1835,
a three story brick building, probably 117 Lake street, was
erected, and finished in the fall, and then filled with goods
by Breese and Shepherd. It was the general impression that
the stand was too *far from the centre* of business, and would
prove a bad speculation.

Mr. Brown has been a professor of religion in connection
with the Presbyterian Church for many years. He sustained
the office of ruling elder in that connection in Vandalia, and
has held the office from 1835, or nearly the entire period of
his residence in this city; and is as well acquainted with eccle-
siastical, as with legal business. He has constantly been a
stanch supporter of his own branch of the church; and a reliable helper in any thing properly claiming his aid in any other
connection.

The first church edifice of the Presbyterian connection was erected upon the alley on Clark Street; between Lake and Randolph, on the West side of the street, (54 Clark street,) where the firm of S. H. Kerfoot & Co. are now situated. The building fronted towards Lake St.; and a large slough run diagonally through the lot in front of the Church, which, on rainy Sabbaths, and in wet times, was bridged by benches from the Church. The writer of this, has a distinct recollection of thus reaching the interior of this place of worship. This church, was at the time, the only one erected by any denomination; though the Baptists; Methodists, and Episcopalians, all had a church organization; and the Catholics had a small Chapel near the corner of Washington Street and Michigan Avenue. A few families lived on the north side of the river, and a few stores of goods had been opened there. The town had no sidewalks; and mud of no very certain depth, was plenty, and easily reached. Nothing like a harbor existed; and vessels were accustomed to lie outside, and unload by lighters.

In 1840, Mr. Brown was appointed School Agent; an office which involved the care of the funds for School purposes in this city. His election was almost accidental; being by a majority of one only of the Whig party, with which he always acted. His acceptance was on the condition, that his services should be gratuitous; and this very likely contributed to keep him in the office, at a time when party greed watched for every post of profit, however small, very much as hungry dogs watched for bones, without regard to their size, or the sort of animals to which they belong. Perhaps the city never made a more fortunate hit, either by blunder or design; for the state of our Schools hitherto had been most deplorable. The School Fund was all unproductive; having been let, for the most part, to parties who had failed to pay, either principal or interests. There were no school-houses fit for use, and the whole matter of Schools was in a decidedly helter-skelter condition. The real era of a change dates with the election of Mr. Brown to this office of School Agent. Confidence began at once to revive; for all parties, even the hungry ones, felt that the fund *was now safe.*

It was no small labor to collect the scattered fragments of the fund, and put them in shape to be productive; but it was accomplished: and though Mr. B. devoted twelve or thirteen years to this business, in connection with his other affairs; loaning it out as it was collected, he never made an uncollectable debt. The Schools gradually assumed tone and character; suitable houses were built, and the system, as it now is, gained shape and consistency.

At the time of his resignation of the office of School Agent, in view of his gratuitous services, the Common Council of the city, passed the following resolutions:

" *Whereas*, In the resignation of Wm. H. Brown, late School Agent, the community have lost the services of a faithful, diligent, and meritorious officer; one who for the long period of thirteen years has bestowed a paternal care—to the fostering and judicious management of that sacred trust—the School Fund; and

Whereas, Although the unsolicited expression of public approbation may not add one iota to the already established character of the individual, who is the object of it; yet we believe that a testimonial, of this nature, may afford to any honorable mind a feeling of pleasure and gratification on retiring from office, with the unbiased verdict of well done thou good and faithful servant.

Thereupon be it resolved by the Mayor and Aldermen of the City of Chicago in Common Council assembled.

That we tender to Wm. H. Brown, late School Agent, our fullest expression of respect and approbation, for the correct and judicious manner in which, for such a long period of years, he has fulfilled the duties appertaining to his late position.

Resolved, That in the economical execution and careful attention, with which the late agent has performed his official requirements, we have presented, for the future guidance of his successor, an example well worthy of imitation; and in which we discern the very unusual occurrence of a public office being held by one individual for so long a period, more for the promotion of a laudable and praisworthy object, than for the emoluments attached to it.

Resolved, That for the more fully carrying out the intention of this Preamble and Resolutions, they be entered on record, and a copy presented to the subject of them."

Mr. B. was one of the first Inspectors of Common Schools, elected under the city charter; and was in that Board for twelve or thirteen consecutive years. This Board of inspectors has been the instrument and agency, and in good degree the cause of our present School System. He was a constant and punctual attendant at its sittings, and a leading and influential member of it; and is entitled to his share of the credit of what it has done.

In the winter of 1846, in connection with a few others, Mr. Brown purchased the original charter of the Galena and Chicago Union Rail Road, from the Estate of E. K. Hubbard, Esq., then lately deceased. Measures were immediately taken to put on foot a working Railroad in the Northwest. A little piece of road had been built before Mr. Hubbard's death, but it was never worked, and went to decay. To start this Galena Road was an undertaking of no small labor. The country was poor: there were no Rail Roads anywhere in the West; and nobody had much faith in them, nor in fact in anything else. So completely had all confidence been wrecked, in the great revulsions of 1836, and onward, that nobody was willing to embark in any new scheme, either with effort or capital. The extent to which this was then true, cannot be conceived of now, by those who have no experience in that chapter of our history. This Galena Road was therefore looked upon as a very doubtful affair; and any amount of writing and cyphering, conventioning and speech-making, was necessary to get it started. The farmers in the country, who had felt in all their bones, as well as pockets, the need of some means of getting to market with their crops, were much more alive to it than our city property holders; who had saved what little they had out of the fire, so to speak; and who did not like to risk it again beyond their fingers' ends. But the farmers were poor and able to take but little stock; and as the citizens would not risk much, the road was begun on a rather small scale. Mr. B. became one of the largest sub-scribers to the stock, and is yet one of the most extensive of its stockholders. He has always been a Director of the Road, and is now its Vice-President. He has therefore had ample opportunity to aid in giving shape to the policy under which that Road has been managed.

Mr. Brown was the very man to have a hand in that under-taking. Cautious to a degree verging on excess: knowing the full value of every dollar that passes through his hands: and constitutionally determined that every dime shall do its own duty, he was the very man to aid in the beginning of a road, without adequate means and without confidence, and carry it forward, step by step, to successs. The first twelve miles of the road only cost about $6000 per mile; but the first twelve miles told the story, for they showed that the road could be built, and would pay. This road has been the goose that has laid our golden eggs. It is the mother of all the rest in our Northwest.

Mr. B. is a man of capital. He had acquired a competency before his removal to this city, and since that time, with the exception of the perilous years succeeding 1836, has been con-stantly adding to the amount. He early became possessed of considerable tracts of real estate, which has of late, very rapidly enhanced in value. He has entered into no rash speculations, nor made any desperate pushes for fortune. He takes care of what he has; and adds to it when he can do so with safety. He has never entered so largely upon building as have some others, but has expended considerable sums in that way at one time and another. His late residence, at the N-W. cor. of Pine and Illinois Streets, North Side, he erected at a cost of ten thousand dollars, in 1836; and it was, at that time, considered the best house in the city. He is now building a residence, with front of Athens marble, on Michigan Avenue, to cost about thirty thousand dollars. As to his present possessions, he is not a man who makes any exhibition of his property. His answer to a question regarding it, was, that the inquirer would have "to guess as to the amount." Our guess therefore is, that it will not fall below $500,000, and may go to twice that sum, or even above that.

Mr. Brown is personally a tall, well-formed man, with a slight stoop of the shoulders; with a keen dark eye, and hair once black as the raven, but now inclining to iron-gray. When young, he is said to have been a very fine-looking man, and we can well believe it, for he holds his honors very well as yet.

Mr. Brown is a *giving* man; being applied to, perhaps, in aid of more charities than any one man in the city; and perhaps he answers to as many, or more, than any man. But he is not *naturally* a giver, for his *motto* is, to keep what he has: and his native answer to all applications, when that answer does not flow through the channel of his christian principles, would very likely be his easy *No!* His manner is often *brusque;* but his heart is kindly; and though he who comes to him for an object not wholly explained, may be chilled by the perpendicularities of a nervous impatience, which explodes suddenly: he has only to wait for the flow of kindness and good sense, which is sure to come, to be reassured.

Mr. Brown has the talent of good common sense; one most certainly of which the world has need, as fully as of any other; this, with his inflexible integrity, gives him a position in regard to trusts, both public and private, held by few men in our city. He is now in the midst of well ripened middle life, and yet in active duty—a large part of it connected with these trusts, of various kinds, put into his hands. We say of him, as Horace said of Augustus—we forget the Latin of it—but the meaning of it is, "Late may he go hence."

Mr. Brown died in Amsterdam, Holland, June 17, 1867, aged 72 years.

BENJAMIN W. RAYMOND, ESQ.

[From the Chicago Magazine, April, 1857.]

Late in the seventeenth century, a few Huguenots, driven from France by persecution to England, settled afterwards in New England. The subject of this sketch is a descendant from these, on his father's side. He was born in Rome, Oneida county, New York, in 1801; and was the son of Benjamin Raymond, who, as early as 1796, left his birth-place, Richmond, Berkshire county, Mass. His mother was a daughter of Thomas Wright, one of the brothers of that name who, emigrating from Weathersfield, Conn., were among the first settlers of Rome, which was long known as Wright's Settlement, in the wilderness of the then West. His father was engaged for some years in connection with the late Judge Wright, (afterwards chief engineer of the Erie canal,) in surveying into townships the northern counties of New York; and which were then all a wilderness, from the Mohawk River northward to the St. Lawrence. He selected the site of the town of Potsdam, in St. Lawrence county, where he lived for several years, and where he held the office of Judge for the county. He died in 1824, in the state of Delaware; being then engaged as engineer upon the Delaware and Chesapeake Canal.

The early years of Benjamin W. were spent with an aunt in Whitestown, New York, having lost his mother at the age of five years. When he had reached the age of ten, he was taken home to pursue his education in an academy which his father had established; having erected, at his own expense, a building to be used for the purpose of a high school and of public worship. Here he spent four years, dividing his time between school and the duties of a clerk in a village store. He also spent a good part of a year at school in Montreal, boarding with a French family where no English was spoken.—Afterwards he resumed his clerkship at his father's store, in Norfolk, St. Lawrence Co., and wound up his school attendance in the study of practical mathematics, particularly surveying, which he afterwards practiced to some extent.

His introduction to the more responsible cares of business took place at the age of nineteen, when he was sent down the Ratchett River, into the St. Lawrence, to Montreal, with a large quantity of lumber, which he was to sell and account for, and in which he acquitted himself to the full satisfaction of his employer. About two years after this, he purchased a small stock of goods, and commenced business on his own account: but his father dying soon after, he was left, at the age of 22, the eldest of nine orphan children, without other means of support than his small stock of goods, purchased on credit, and sold, of necessity, under all the disadvantages of a new country without currency, or other means of purchase; and dependant on a barter of crude commodities for whatever trade was done. As his eldest brother was but thirteen years of age, he soon saw the impossibility of sustaining the family at Norfolk, and so closed his business at that place, in debt to his largest creditor to the amount of $600, (which was paid in instalments some years afterwards), and started for Oneida county, once more to try a new tack for his life voyage. Here, a clerkship introduced him to a partnership in business with Mr. Wm. Wright, one of the oldest merchants at Rome, which was continued for three years. A feeling of responsibility on account of his orphan brothers and sisters induced habits of the strictest industry and economy, and led him to adopt those principles of temperance to which he has ever since adhered. The circle of young men into which he had been thrown in St. Lawrence county were dissipated, and their gayety was not without a charm for young Raymond. But when returning to Oneida county he firmly resolved to leave all such associates behind, and to seek for the future only the society of the strictly virtuous. Temperance societies were not yet invented; but Mr. Raymond made a pledge for himself, and has kept it to this day.

It was here, during the great revival of religion, in which Rev. C. G. Finney figured as the chief preacher, that Mr. Raymond made a profession of religion, early in the year 1826.

One of the first Young Mens' Temperance Societies in the State was formed at Rome, and Mr. Raymond at once relinquished the sale of liquors, though it was a very important source of profit to the merchant at that time. That was in 1828

In 1831, Mr. Raymond formed his first acquaintance with his future friend and partner, Hon. S. N. Dexter; and very soon after turned his steps westward, determined to seek his fortune in what was then the *far west;* with a promise from Mr. Dexter that if he should find a good place near the western lakes for settlement and trade, he would supply him the capital necessary for a commencement of business. In this journey he pushed westward through northern Ohio and Michigan, as far as White Pigeon; the last twenty-five miles of which was reached on the back of an Indian pony, guided partly by lead of an Indian trail, and partly by the course of the sun. He found plenty of persons who, like himself, were in search of places for the sale of goods, but very few who promised to be

purchasers, and so turned backward as far as the town of East
Bloomfield, in Western New York, where he once more commenced business. Here he spent four years in a successful
trade, connected with the purchase of wool. Here, also, one of
the most important steps of his life was taken, in his entrance
into the matrimonial relation with Miss Amelia Porter, of East
Bloomfield, his present wife; a step which has probably had as
much to do with his success in life, and the position he now
occupies, as any other. Mrs. Raymond was the mother of two
sons, one only living, and now a professor in Williams College.

Finding that his business did not allow of much expansion
at East Bloomfield, he began, in 1835, to look once more westward, and Chicago being then somewhat talked about, he at
once fixed his attention upon this place, being confirmed in the
idea, from its natural position upon the map, that it would at
some time be a place of importance; and also from a remark he
once heard from Hon. De Witt Clinton; whose sagacity in
regard to such matters was seldom at fault.

In January, 1836, he therefore set out by stage for Chicago,
being provided with authority to draw upon his friend Dexter
to the amount of $10,000, if he chose to do so, for purposes of
joint investment in real estate. After some looking at Milwaukee and elsewhere, and investing his $10,000, he returned,
closed up his business in N. Y., and set his stake in Chicago
about the 1st of June, 1836; having been preceded by a large
stock of goods; which, however, having to go by sail vessels
around the Lakes, did not arrive until July. The city was at
that time running over with merchandise, wanting nothing but
purchasers. Such a class of merchants, too, as were a portion of
them, never seen elsewhere: being mere adventurers, who had,
by hook or by crook, and commonly by both, got possession of
their stocks; their next aim was to get rid of them at whatever
price could be had.

This disheartening and ruinous condition of things, left but a
poor chance for him who thought only of a legitimate trade,
which should turn his stock into cash.—Mr. R. was therefore
obliged to look about him for other avenues to help off his
goods. He established a branch at Milwaukee, one at Geneva,
in Kane Co., and another at DesPlaines, on the Canal.

The disasters of that period, commencing in August, 1836,
were under full headway for about three years, and came especially upon such as had made purchases of real estate, with notes
to mature from time to time. The fall of 1837 found the firm
of B. W. Raymond & Co. minus the ability to meet their en-
gagements by about $15,000, in addition to their loss of capital,
amounting to as many more. This was a state of things with a
bad look to it, and was fully made known to his partner; but
Mr. Dexter was a man with a back bone in him, and nobly sustained the house with $20,000, as it was called for, during the

years 1837–8–9; so that, by attention to meeting and securing liabilities as they accrued, the credit of the house was unshaken and their business uninterrupted during the whole period of that terrible depression. From the year 1838 to 1843, business was good, and the firm had so far retrieved its condition that Mr. Raymond determined to make an effort to put himself square with the world again.

For this purpose he sold out his stock of goods, receiving one-half in cash and in paper running six months, and the balance in real estate. This latter consisted of sixty feet on Clark street, including the old Post Office on the alley of the Sherman House Block, which was valued at $5000. By this sale, and by collecting dues, and by turning over all his interest in the real estate owned by the firm, to his partner, who was the largest creditor—Post Office property and all, at its estimated value, the whole precisely paid the liabilities of B. W. Raymond & Co., with 7 per cent. interest, together with all the private debts of Mr. Raymond; and left him with about $2000 for a fresh start. Mr. Dexter rather objected to receiving all the real estate in their hands, as it had begun again to advance, and he was anxious that Mr. Raymond should share in the profit, as well as to have borne the labor. But Mr. R. preferred to have his affairs in a shape to leave his family with some resources in case of his death; and, besides, he wished to have one more clear start in the world. Mr. Dexter would, however, only receive the property on condition that Mr. Raymond should manage it as he had done, and gave him full power of attorney to that effect. After all transfers were made, Mr. D. so arranged matters as that an exact account should be kept of all real estate to him, with 7 per cent. added each year, and then that all profits over the cost and interest should be equally divided between Mr. R. and himself; as his intention, he declared to be, that Mr. R. should not spend seven of the best years of his life exclusively for his benefit; but that if anything was to be made from real estate, he should share it.

Previous to the year 1843, Mr. R. purchased, on account of Mr. D. and himself, of the late Jas. T. Gifford, one-half of his interest in the village of Elgin, and in that year commenced the erection of a woolen factory for Mr. Dexter, which was completed in 1844. He was also concerned in a store at that place till 1851, and owned considerable real estate in the town.

In the year 1839, he purchased the lot No. 122, on Lake street, Chicago, and in connection with Messrs. Strachan & Scott, erected, not the first brick, but the first *fire-proof* stores in the town. In about three weeks after their completion, the great fire of that year swept the whole block on Lake street, from their stores to Dearborn street, including the original Tremont House, standing diagonally across the street from its present position—and northward to the alley.

In March, 1839, Mr. Raymond was put in nomination for Mayor of the city, without any expectation on his part of an election, since party lines were then drawn in regard to city officers, as well as those in the state or nation; and Mr. R. acted with the whigs, while their opponents were largely in the ascendant. He was, however, elected, together with half the Council on the same side, which put upon him the duty of giving a casting vote, whenever the question of office, or appointment, or of party advantage should divide that body. Mr. Raymond acknowledges that for once he was swayed by his friends, who insisted that he ought to use his power for the party to which he belonged: but that on the next day he formed the resolution to which he has since adhered, of never voting for a man whom he deemed unfit, because he was, of a particular party. From that time he has been opposed to bringing party politics into the arena of our municipal elections.

During this year the well-known counterfeiting of the Canal checks of $100 occurred. Mr. Raymond gave such attention to the case that three fellows engaged in the business were put into the clutches of justice; of whom two went to Alton, and the other,* by changing venue, got off on straw bail, and was seen no more in these parts. He brought up in Sing Sing, however, and may be doing service to the state of New York till this day, for aught known of him.

The Mayor, at this time, was paid a nominal salary of $1000, which, by depreciation of city orders, in which it was paid, reduced it to about $750. Mr. R. made no money from his office, however; for that year being one of great suffering on the line of the canal, the occupants of the shanties naturally poured into the city for relief; and the salary, drawing after it more of the same sort, went to the aid of the Emeralders, as much more has gone since; not only from the plethoric pockets of Mayors, but from all other pockets reachable, by lugubrious jeremiads of want.

There came on, also, during the year, a great bridge contest. That over the river at Dearborn street being swept away, a strong party arose opposing the erection of another, thinking, either that those who wanted to get from that side of the stream to this, might crawl under; or, that people who would leave the "sunny south" side and banish themselves to those hyperborean regions lying to the northward of the current of mud, ought to stay there, and no more trouble those of so much better taste, and of better fortunes. So strong was this utterance of the *vox populi* that the matter was decided in that *com-*

* The genuine scrip was printed in the *Chicago American* office, and was an exceedingly poor job. Only a poor printer could have executed the counterfeit; the type, vignette—a ship—and the paper could be found in any country printing-office. The counterfeiter tried here was the notorious Otis Allen, of Buffalo, N.Y.

mon council by the casting vote of the Mayor, and a bridge obtained on Clark street, on condition that the north-siders should subscribe $3000 of city bonds to put it over. And so the benighted hyperboreans were admitted once more to sunlight and the society of "the people."

The sale of Fort Dearborn addition to Chicago took place during that year. Mr. R. had the first intimation of it while in New York, in April; and as he knew from the history of like cases, that the people of Chicago expected the lands to be given to the city, as had been customary, he exerted himself for a postponement of the sale, till the matter could be brought before Congress—the sale being advertised by Mr. Van Buren, the President, to take place in June. For this purpose he visited Washington, and saw the President, who put him off with the soft ambiguities which he knew so well how to use; and as soon as he was gone, hurried on the sale, under the averment that the government was "in pressing need of funds." As the next best thing, Mr. R., with a committee of the council, put in for a public square, consisting of a block, to be reserved from sale.

Their success was better than nothing, inasmuch as they got half what they asked for; and Dearborn Park testifies to-day the result. He also persuaded the Agent of the Government to add 60 feet to the width of State Street, for a market.

As a sample of celerity of travel in those days, Mr. R. started, in the month of March, 1839, for New York. He left on Tuesday morning, by stage; that is, in a lumber wagon with trunks for seats, and after riding day and night, with one night's exception, brought up at Tecumseh, forty miles from Detroit, at three o'clock on the next Sunday morning, the last seven miles being on foot, as the four horses were sufficiently loaded by the aforesaid trunks and wagon. During one week more of travel, beginning on the following Monday, Buffalo was gained; and one week further still brought them to New York, making three weeks in the transit. Eight years after this voyage of three weeks, Mr. Raymond was laughed at for saying, that in ten years more, he expected to make the same journey in three days. Perhaps the laughers are cachinnating yet.

In 1842, Mr. Raymond was once more elected Mayor of Chicago. This was about the time of the expiration of the long depression which commenced in 1837. City orders were still hawking about at 70 to 75 cents on the dollar, for goods or truck of some sort; and the people were as poor as the city. Real estate had but little value, and everybody would have been rid of it but that nobody else would take it; and so being obliged to keep what they had, an abundance of people were made rich in time in spite of themselves.

The city government entered upon a rigid course of economy; their whole expenditures for the year municipal, 1842, were about $9800, and the receipts $13,800, about $4000 more than the expenditures, and before the end of the year, city orders loomed up to par.

During the year, the late cemetery grounds were selected; the old burying grounds being among the sand hills near Lill's brewery. Some forty acres of those grounds were bought, surveyed, and a public sale had. To get means of paying for the forty acres, some $1200 of city script was pledged in a loan of $600 for sixty days! The sale furnished the means to redeem the script. This will, perhaps, seem small business at this day, but a great many large things begin small.

During the next year, 1843, Mr. R. endeavored to induce some of his creditors to take the lot on Clark street, north of the Sherman House, and including the old Post office, at $5-000 in discharge of liabilities. This idea was scouted, and the property was passed over to his partner as already stated. He kept it till it brought him $19,500, and it could not be had to-day, probably, for less than $60,000.

When the Galena Railroad was started, Mr. R. was fully ready to enter into it, with all the means and influence he could command. As one of its first Board of Directors he pledged almost his entire capital, in connection with other Directors, for the purchase of the first iron to build its track, and in connection with John B. Turner, Esq., then acting Director, afterwards President, negotiated the sale of the first issue of bonds of the Road in eastern cities, which, at that day (1848), was not an easy matter, while Wall street was well supplied with Illinois State Bonds, interest unpaid. The first sales were only made to confidential friends, who relied upon their representations, as capitalists generally had no confidence in any western enterprise.

In consequence of the success of that enterprise, and its beneficial effects upon the country and city, he entered upon active efforts to build the road known as the Fox River Valley Railroad, now called Elgin and State Line Branch of the North-Western. The construction of this road was somewhat delayed, owing to the great number of such enterprises on foot at once, and the failure of some of the more unimportant ones, but it is now finished, and in operation from Elgin to Geneva Lake.

Mr. Raymond, though in comfortable circumstances, is not one of the wealthy men of the city; for he has never worshipped the "Golden Calf." His aim has never been to make the most money. Hence, he has commonly sold out any considerable tracts of real estate in his hands, and used the money to advance objects of public use and benefit. He also gives largely and freely. Perhaps no man in our midst more fully realizes the pleasure of a deed of benevolence which costs something, than he. No man of his long residence and various experiences with all sorts of men in public and private life, has fewer

2

enemies, or more fully commands the public confidence. The trust in his entire integrity of character is full and universal. He has only to believe a thing right to be induced to act accordingly, without question or delay. He is a man of about five feet ten inches in height, with light hair and a blonde complexion. His words are few, in low tones, and his demeanor quiet; the aspect is that of amiability and harmony of character.

He was a Director of the old Hydraulic company, (which first supplied water to the city,) from its beginning to its close; is now a Director in the Gas & Coke Co., and was for many years a Director of the pioneer railroad of the west, the Galena & Chicago Union Rail Road.

He, as President, obtained the Charter for the Old Ladies' Home, of Chicago, and has been connected with the Board of Trustees, as President or Treasurer, since its organization; and Treasurer of the Old People's Home.

He was one of the originators of the City of Lake Forest; obtained the Charter for the Lake Forest University, and was President of the Board of Trustees, for the first twelve years; and still a member of the Board of Trustees; also, a member of the Board of Trustees of Beloit College; and Rockford Female Seminary. In 1864, he, as President, with the aid of a few friends, organized and obtained the Charter for the Elgin National Watch Company, and procured subscriptions to the Stock; he is still connected with the Company as a Director: having resgned the Presidency in favor of a younger and more active man—T. M. Avery, Esq.

Elgin is most indebted to Mr. Raymond for its early and later prominence. He made large investments there; and furnished the material for many of the most important enterprises. His contributions for the establishment of their Academy were liberal; he was one of the first, and for many years, their leading merchant, having placed there, in 1838, the largest stock of goods west of Chicago. He was a partner in the foundry of Adams & Co., the first manufacturers of corn-shellers in the West; he was chiefly instrumental in the establishment of the woolen factory built by S. N. Dexter, Esq., in 1842—the first woolen factory in the State of Illinois; he assisted in the erection of a large tannery; and, lastly, and of greater importance than all the rest, as President of the National Watch Company.

Mr. R.'s political views are Republican; but he regards strict moral character, integrity, and capability above party consideration.

Mr. R. is a consistent member of the second Presbyterian Church, and has held the office of Ruling Elder in it since its organization in 1842.

His health is pretty uniformly good, and the hope of his friends is to see him useful a long while yet.

HON. J. YOUNG SCAMMON.

[From the Chicago Magazine, March, 1857.]

The subject of this sketch was born in Whitfield, Lincoln Co., Maine, in the year 1812. His father was the Hon. Eliakim Scammon, of East Pittston, Kennebec Co., Maine, a man widely known and universally esteemed, and who, for many successive years, represented his town and county in both branches of the Legislature of that State.

Mr. Scammon's mother was the daughter of David Young, one of the first settlers, and most wealthy men in East Pittston. Mr. Young was a prominent man in the community in which he lived. As a Jeffersonian Republican, he often represented his town in the General Court of Massachussetts, Maine having formed a part of Massachussetts until the year 1820, when it was admitted into the Union as a separate State.

Mr. Scammon, from childhood, has had a fondness for agricultural and horticultural pursuits. He would have been a farmer, were it not that an accident deprived him, at the age of 10 years, of the full use of his left hand. Though this probably changed his occupation in life, it did not diminish his natural love for the cultivation of the soil, or destroy his taste for the beautiful and perfect, in all that relates to this truly noble occupation. When he resided at the corner of Michigan Ave. and Randolph Street, he had the finest garden to be seen in the city, at that time; and he now preserves his beautiful garden.

Mr. Scammon received his literary education at the Maine Wesleyan Seminary, Lincoln Academy, and Waterville College. He read law in Hallowell, in his native State; he was admitted to the bar in Kennebec Co., and immediately after started upon a tour of the States. He arrived at Chicago, in September, 1835, upon a cold and stormy day. He made the then somewhat more than unpleasant and hazardous passage of the lakes, in the old steamboat, Pennsylvania, which at that early period made a trip from Buffalo, by the way of Green Bay, to Chicago. On the passage of the steamboat from Green Bay to this city, a furious storm arose, compelling her to put into Washington Harbor, near Death's Door, at the north end of Lake Michigan. Here she lay until the storm abated; provisions running out, and the passengers being put on a short allowance, in the meantime. Taking a fresh start from Washington Harbor, the storm again

raged fearfully, and there was great apprehension of shipwreck
among the passengers and crew.

Arrived at Chicago, the steamer was compelled to anchor outside the bar, there being no entrance to the harbor, except for
vessels of a very small size. The passengers were landed in a
boat, and made their way from the beach up to the old Sauganash Hotel, in a driving rain, through the tall prairie grass and
deep mud. They found the hotel crowded, and a very large
number of the inmates sick with the bilious fever. In fact, altogether, a more dismal and dreary aspect the town could not
have presented. Coming from the beautiful hills of New England, and their bracing and healthy air, the town appeared to
the new comer to be almost a dismal swamp; and his first impression was anything but favorable to a location in it.

Mr. Scammon had letters to Mr. Henry Moore, who was then
an attorney in the town, and deputy of Col. Richard J. Hamilton, Clerk of the Courts of the County of Cook. In a few days,
the weather cleared off, and almost as soon the mud disappeared
and there succeeded one of those beautiful Indian summers with
which the West is so highly favored. Just as Mr. S. was about
to leave town, to continue his journey southward, Mr. Moore
called upon him, and stated that the Circuit Court had just
commenced its session; that his own business prevented his
giving further assistance to Col. Hamilton, and that the gentleman that Col. Hamilton had employed in his place had been
attacked with fever. He asked Mr. S. if he would not assist
Col. H. during the term of Court. This was regarded by Mr. S.
as a fine opportunity to become acquainted with the mode of
practice and the forms of legal proceedings in Illinois, and was
at once accepted. He accordingly assisted Col. H. through
the term; who finding that he was ready and at home in the
performance of the duties of Clerk, proposed to make him his
deputy, and, at the same time, allow him to "hang out his
shine" in the Clerk's office.

In those days, rooms for offices were not plenty in Chicago,
and the lawyers, being mostly bachelors, lodged in their offices.
Mr. S. had endeavored in vain to find an eligible office, so he
accepted Col. H.'s proposal, and established his office in the
"North-east Corner" of the Clerk's office, from which it was
separated, not as often in early times in the West, were the
places of the Bar, the Court, and Jury, by chalk or coal lines,
but by an imaginary one.

Col. H. then held about every office in Cook County which
he could legally hold. He was Judge of Probate, Clerk of the
Circuit Court, Clerk of the County Commissioners' Court, School
Commissioner, Recorder of Deeds, Notary Public, and Bank
Commissioner. All these were held in a small Grecian build-
ing, erected on the north-east corner of the Court House Square,

which was subsequently lengthened, and transformed into a Court House.

Mr. S.'s days were spent in this room, in the study of his profession and attending to the duties of clerk for Col. H. At night, he lodged like other young men, in the same office. As he made acquaintances his business increased, and in 1836, he entered into a copartnership with Buckner S. Morris. They continued together for eighteen months, and did a large and successful business. They then dissolved, and Mr. Scammon practiced alone for a year or more, when he formed a connection with Norman B. Judd, the partnership lasting until 1847, when Mr. Scammon becoming greatly interested in the building of the Galena & Chicago Union Railroad, and wishing to give much of his time to railroad matters, he and Mr. Judd dissolved their connection, though they continued to occupy the same office.

When Mr. Scammon came to Chicago, it was a time of almost universal speculation. Nearly every one was rich; at least in prospect. He was solicited to speculate, but declined, on the ground that he liked his profession, and should be happier in practicing it than in attempting to make a fortune by speculating. He thus was enabled to devote his time faithfully and unremittingly to the practice of his profession. His industry and promptness in paying over to his clients all monies collected —somewhat of a virtue in the early days of Western life—won him the favor of the community, both at home and abroad, and his practice soon became large and commanding. This favor, obtained by faithfulness and probity in the discharge of his business transactions, in the outset of his professional career, has been of great benefit to him in after life, and, no doubt, to it, to a very great extent, he owes the credit which he now enjoys in Chicago, as well as the Eastern cities.

Indeed, Mr. Scammon has made it a leading principle, in all his business transactions, to promise nothing that he could not perform, and to work with the greatest possible zeal and ardor to secure the completion of that which he promised. His credit as a banker he regards as above every other consideration, both of profit and present standing; and he would sacrifice all he possesses to preserve that untarnished. The business public are aware of this, and hence put great confidence in any monied institution with which he is connected.

Mr. Scammon has made great efforts to obtain a safe and reliable banking law in this State, which would be the means of preventing a recourse to the system of what is called "Wild Cat Banking," by which a number of irresponsible institutions are got up in neighboring States and Territories, for the purpose of circulating their irresponsible and irredeemable paper here. The law, as it heretofore stood, restrained and restricted the home banker, while it gave free license to the foreign institutions, which are responsible to no one, and which, at best, depend wholly upon the ability, or rather inclination, of the owners to redeem their promises. Mr. S. has endeavored to make our banking system of that character which would invite the capital of the best business men of this and other States for investment, at the same time that it would possess such guards and restrictions as would secure the public in the most perfect manner. Mr. S. has worked long and faithfully to this end, and hopes finally to be able to accomplish an object which has been one of the leading purposes of his life. The feeling against banking of all kinds which exists in some portions of the State, and which has been taken advantage of by the advocates of irresponsible banking in the northern part, has hitherto been the great obstacle with which Mr. S. has had to contend; but he hopes, in time, and by the aid of the growing intelligence and good sense of the people, to succeed in perfecting such a system of banking as will be a credit to the State, and of the utmost advantage to its inhabitants.

In 1837, without solicitation on his part, Mr. Scammon was selected as the Attorney of the State Bank of Illinois; and in 1839, he was appointed Reporter of the Supreme Court of the State, which office he continued to hold till 1845, when he resigned, on account of the press of his business at home. He was the first Reporter in this State that ever published a volume, and his books introduced an entirely new era in Western Reports. They were brought out in a style inferior to none, and superior to most of the reports in the Eastern States.

The writer might here probably state, that Mr. Scammon has ever taken a lively interest in public affairs. While being indefatigably occupied with the management of his private business, he has not allowed himself to be wholly engrossed in the labors necessarily incident to men of large and accumulative means, but has been, in one way or another, connected with most of the great leading undertakings associated with the progress of our state and city. He has, in fact, been among the foremost in contributing to the development of the resources of Illinois, and the advancement of the interests of Chicago and the surrounding country. A New Churchman or Swedenborgian in religion, which includes all great measures of useful and beneficient progress he is himself progressive in sentiment, and conservative in practice. His motto is, and always has been, at least as long as the writer of this has known him, "Conservative Progress." Still into whatever undertaking he enters, he throws himself with his whole soul, and with all his might; and whenever he undertakes a project, he is indefatigable and preserving, until it is accomplished.

To the Hon. William B. Ogden and Mr. Scammon are the public specially indebted for the commencement of the Galena & Chicago Railroad. After the railroad enterprises which had their inception in 1837, had failed, and were abandoned, and all confidence in Illinois was lost by capitalists, when hope was nearly dead in the minds of our people; Messrs. Ogden and Scammon counselled together upon the subject of railroads, and the Galena Railroad in particular. To induce the Michigan Central Railroad, which then hardly reached New Buffalo, to come to Chicago, and thus aid in extending railroad lines farther West, Messrs. O. and S. went to Indiana, and spent much time in getting hold of and reviving the charter of the Buffalo and Mississippi Railroad, which possessed the sole power of building a road from Michigan City to Illinois State Line, in the direction of Chicago. They had previously, on the opening of books for the road, traveled over the entire distance between Chicago and Galena, holding meetings, making speeches, and procuring subscriptions to the stock of the Galena Road. They were themselves among the largest stockholders in the Company, and by their exertions and personal pledges of fidelity to the interests of the stockholders, they obtained stock enough to commence operations in the road; and it is not claiming too much to say, that but for them this great pioneer road in the West would not have been commenced till many years later.

In the commencement of the building of this road, Mr. Scammon devoted a large portion of his time, gratuitously, to the project. He familiarized himself with the details of the transactions of the Company, and kept a strict watch upon its operations. Besides, to sustain the credit of the Company, he borrowed money more than once upon his individual name, and loaned it to the Treasurer, when the road had not sufficient credit to obtain an additional accommodation from its banker; nor even the confidence of a majority of its Directors, in their ability to go on with their enterprise. But the faith of the subject of our sketch was full and unwavering. Indeed, so great were the difficulties, and so numerous the disappointments in the outset of the operations of this Company, to which Chicago is indebted for so much of its material prosperity, that at one time, during the absence of Mr. Ogden, all the Directors, with the exception of Mr. Scammon, the late James H. Collins, Esq., and Charles Walker, Esq., appeared discouraged at the prospect of affairs.

 The labors and difficulties attending the early days of the history of this enterprise can hardly be realized at the present time. The country was poor; there was no surplus money in it; subscriptions to the stock of the Company could only be obtained in very small quantities; of eighteen hundred shareholders, the larger number held single, or not more than two or three shares each; while all the shares which were taken were subscribed for, not with a view to profit on the stock, but solely to aid in the enterprise. Mr. S. was one of the largest stock-

holders from the commencement of the undertaking, and when
great efforts were requisite to keep up the credit of the Company, and to prevent its stock from greatly depreciating, he purchased freely of it, and was, by this means, at one time its largest
stockholder. With a view, also, of procuring Eastern aid, he
'proceeded in company with Mr. Ogden, to Boston, and had an
interview with Eastern capitalists. There was at that period
so little confidence in the West or Western enterprises, that
they were very cooly told by one of the largest railroad proprietors in New England, that "Statistics amount to very little
in influencing us. You must go home, raise what money you
can, and when you can get no farther, come to us, and give us
what you have done, and we will take hold of your road and
complete it. You can afford to do this, the road will be of such
immense advantage to your country." Mr. S. determined, upon
the instant, that these prophetic wishes should not be fulfilled.
He returned home, and by his exertions and caution contribued
not a little to that careful management of the road, which ulti-
mated in the success of the enterprise, and in establishing, in
the minds of capitalist everywhere, the ability of Illinois men
to build and manage railroads.

The success of the Galena and Chicago Union Railroad is
the parent of all subsequent railroad movements in this State.
Had that enterprise failed, Chicago would not now count half
its present population.

In the very momentous matter, to the present and succeeding
generations, of establishing the free school system of Illinois,
Mr. Scammon bore a very prominent and important part. There
was no provision for absolutely free schools in Illinois when
Mr. Scammon removed to the State, and for years thereafter.
It required a great struggle to get through the Legislature a
special law for Chicago, authorizing the establishment of
schools by the Town; and the law was only passed on condition that it would be submitted to a vote of the people, before it became operative. When the vote was taken in 1836,
the law was voted down. Its defeat at that time was probably
caused by the large number of unmarried men, the greater part
of whom were speculators in real estate, who were unwilling
to have their property taxed for, as they alleged, the benefit
of other people's children.

Mr. Scammon took an active part in getting up the first charter of the City of Chicago. It was partly through his efforts
that provision for our present free school system was made in
it. The schools first established under it were not, however,
sustained by public opinion. There were few children in the
town, most of its population being young people, and little
interest was felt in the subject. The schools had thus but a
sickly existence, and were of very little value.

Mr. Scammon was appointed one of the Board of School

Inspectors in 1839. The free schools were then so nearly extinct, that it was determined to suspend them, until they could be re-commenced under more favorable auspices, and upon a more stable foundation. Mr. S. took hold of the subject in earnest. He drafted new Ordinances and Laws for the regulation and government of the school system, which were passed; and through him and his co-laborers in the Board of School Inspectors, the system of Common Schools, which has been so successful, and of such incalculable benefit to our City, was established on a broad and permanent basis. He remained in the Board of School Inspectors till 1845, when he was elected an Alderman for the First Ward. His election to this office was opposed by some citizens, who feared he was in favor of too extensive a system in public schools. The first school-house — the brick edifice Nos. 81—7 Madison street, east of Dearborn street — had been built under the direction of the Board of School Inspectors, in 1844. Much complaint had been made by residents of the North and West Divisions of the City, at the large expenditure; very many persons residing in the South Division, also denounced the cost of the construction of such a building as extravagant. Mr. S. determined to secure as large a vote as possible, in order to satisfy the public that "big school-houses" were not unpopular. The consequence was, he received more votes, and was elected by a larger majority, than any Alderman, up to that time, had ever received in the City.

When the new Council was inaugurated, the Mayor recommended that the "big school-house" should be sold, or converted into an "Insane Asylum," and one more suitable to the size and wants of the City be built. It was supposed by the Mayor, that so large a school-house would not be required by the City for a dozen years. Mr. S. was appointed Chairman of the Committee on Schools, in the new Council, and immediately brought forward an ordinance for building a large brick school-house on the North side of the river, stating, at the same time, that it was the policy of the Board of School Inspectors to build another, on the West Side, the next year, and to build a new school-house at least every year. The order was adopted by the Council, and the school-house was built. The construction of this house was followed by that of the fine school building on Madison street, on the West Side. Thus a policy was adopted, which has since been continued and improved upon by the successive Boards of School Inspectors, until our Common Schools have reached their present proud position and high state of usefulness.

In any mention of the Common Schools, however, the name of William Jones, Esq., should not be omitted. For years, in their days of trial, he was one of their most devoted and efficient friends. He seconded Mr. Scammon's efforts and labors with great energy and zeal.

Mr. Scammon has always taken a warm and decided interest
in politics. He was a Whig during the existence of that party,
and for many years chairman of its Congressional, County, and
City Committees; and though often solicited, and more than
once nominated for office, he was never a candidate before the
people, except on two occasions—once when elected Alderman,
and in 1848, when he was the Whig candidate for Congress in
this District, which at that time was composed of seventeen
counties, and overwhelmingly Democratic. Mr. S. received a
very flattering vote, carrying the City of Chicago by a considerable majority, although his party in the city must have been in
a minority of more than a thousand votes.

In politics Mr. Scammon also exhibited his progressive pro-
clivities, having been always on the side of freedom and progress in his party. At the same time he was conservative in
his action, preferring present good, when he could obtain it, to
sacrificing everything to the abstract principles of right. For
this reason, though his freesoil sentiments dated back before
the great contest between Clay and Polk in 1844, he preferred
voting for Mr. Clay, to throwing away his vote. In 1848, also,
he advocated the election of General Taylor, knowing there was
no probability of the election of a freesoil candidate, and doubt-
ing the sincerity of purpose of Mr. Van Buren, who was supported by that party. In 1852, he voted for General Scott, although he preferred Judge McLean, who was his choice for
President. In the late contest, he supported Colonel Fremont
with all the ardor he was capable of, sparing neither his time
nor money in the canvass. Mr. S. has always been inflexibly
opposed to the extention of slavery into the territories, and he
endeavored, in every way in his power, to divorce the Whig
Party of this State from the Pro-Slavery measures with which
a large number of its friends seemed willing to suffer it to be
embarrassed. He contended that his policy in this respect was
both just and expedient; and it is due to him to say, that if his
advice had been carried out, the Whig Party in the Northern
portion of the State, at least, and especially in this city, would
not have remained so long in the hopeless minority in which he
found it when he came to reside here. Many who afterwards
claimed to be Seward, or freesoil Whigs, had previously to
their sudden conversion—subsequently to the election of Gen.
Taylor—opposed, with all their strength, the positions which
Mr. S. took, and which had they been accepted and carried out
by the leaders of the party generally, would have placed the
Whig Party in a far better position before the people than it
had ever attained.

Mr. Scammon was also among the first to perceive the tendency to the breaking up of old party lines in the country generally, and particularly in this City and State, preparatory to the
present fusion of all persons and parties opposed to the spread

of slavery. He suggested and procured the writer, many years ago, to furnish a series of articles on the subject, to a neutral paper then published in this city. These articles, and also other measures taken by him, had no small influence in breaking up party lines in the Chicago City Elections, and in the Northern counties of the State. Although a strict party man himself, as long as he could see any great good which the old Whig Party was capable of performing; still he believed in voting for the best men, and in many instances refused to vote for unworthy or incapable nominees of his own party. It may be proper to state in this connection, that Mr. S. from first to last, has always opposed Native Americanism or Know Nothingism, in all its forms and principles. The writer well remembers the indignation of Mr. S. at an article which appeared in a paper in 1844, of which he was one of the editors. He had a portion of the edition of the paper which contained it suppressed immediately; the article gave great offense, however, as it appeared in part of the edition, and was made a great handle of by the Democrats at that time to the injury of the Whigs. Mr. S.'s principles of civil and religious polity are of too broad and comprehensive a character to accept for a moment the narrow and bigoted platform of that party, which of late has had, for a short time, such a prominent position in our National and State politics.

Mr. Scammon, in 1849, re-organized the Chicago Marine and Fire Insurance Company, an institution which had been chartered in 1836, as a monied corporation, but which had suspended business, although it never had suspended payment. He was one of the chief stockholders under the new organization, and the President of the Company. It commenced with a nominal capital of about $35,000, and an actual cash capital of not exceeding $25,000. Under his auspices, as President, the institution has gradually increased its capital, and extended its business, until it has now an actual cash capital of half a million of dollars, and is the largest monied institution in the State.

Mr. Scammon likes to be a pioneer, judging from his past life. He was the first Swedenborgian in Northern Illinois; the first homœopath; and was among the first and most efficient organizers and supporters of the Galena and Chicago Union Railroad. He also established the first bank under the General Banking Law of this State—the Marine Bank of Chicago. He organized the Chicago Society of the New Jerusalem, when it had only three members, one other beside himself and wife. He also organized, in connection with three other gentlemen, the Illinois Association of the same Church, when there were probably not over a dozen Swedenborgians in the whole State.

Mr. Scammon possesses excellent business tact and management, which is evinced not only in his own prosperity, in the accumulation and investment of a large private fortune, but in the success of the many enterprises in which he was one of the pioneers. He was one of the original stockholders of the Galena; Chicago, Burlington, and Quincy, and several other railroads. Though never a speculator, Mr. S. has become wealthy by judicious and prudent business habits. He is at the present time owner of large and productive real estate in the very centre of the business part of our city. His policy has been not to speculate, by running in debt, but to invest his surplus earnings, and thus reap the advantage of the steady rise of property by the growth of the city. To this policy, together with his industry and economy, he owes his present prosperous position, financially speaking. Mr. S. is a great advocate for the singleness of employments, nevertheless, his practice does not conform to his theory in this respect, as he is banker, lawyer, real estate owner, and has a large interest in railroads himself. It has been asserted by some—perhaps those too envious of another's prosperity—that accommodations from the old Illinois State Bank contributed to Mr. S.'s wealth. This is a mistake; he never borrowed a dollar from the bank, or had any accommodations from it, or purchased a foot of land, or other property belonging to it, except at public sale, in competition with others. The only favor the bank ever did him was to select him as its attorney. He had no other connection with it.

In his profession Mr. Scammon has stood deservedly high, and at one time had the most lucrative practice of any lawyer in the city. In fact, he has generally had more business than he could attend to, and of late years, his banking and other matters have demanded so much of his attention, that he has for the last two or three years given little time to his profession. In 1849, he took Mr. Ezra B. McCagg, who had been his confidential law clerk, for two years previously, into partnership, and they have since practiced together. He has always been a friend to young men, and has had a very large number of students in his office. These it has ever been his habit to accustom to the details of practice, thus grounding them well in the most important particulars in the professson. Thus he has been successful, in almost every instance, in making good, practical lawyers of his students. The advantages of the thorough training received by students in the office of Mr. S., is fully indicated by the fact, that of all the young men who have been under his supervision, not more than two have failed to turn out well.

Mr. Scammon, like all men of positive principles, is decided in his opinions, still he is liberal and kind to those who disagree with him. Indeed, a majority of the young men in his office, who have received his assistance, countenance, and support, have been, in political opinions, opposite to himself.

Though Mr. S. has devoted himself for many years so arduously to the law, and also been deeply immersed in business, he has not forgotten his early love for literature and fine arts. He continues still to cultivate it. He writes on political and religious subjects, gives public lectures, etc. In conversation he is entertaining, his information being general and varied, and his desire to impart it, a natural attribute of the man. He reads and speaks several modern languages with fluency, and continues his early study of the classics, to which he has always been drawn by his taste for ancient literature.

Mr. S. is blessed with the companionship of a congenial partner, a lady every way qualified to contribute to his happiness, and an interesting family of children, the oldest grown to a fine-looking young man, who is receiving the benefit of as good an education as his father's means and position can afford.

Mr. S. still continues to work as heretofore, though less in his profession. To the question "Why do you not give up business?" he replied, "I have no right to do so. Use is the central principle of Heaven, and no one can be happy, except in the degree in which he is occupied in some useful employment."

The foregoing sketch of Mr. Scammon's life was printed in 1857, in which year he went to Europe with his family, where his wife died, and her remains were interred at Soden, in Nassau, about ten miles from Frankfort on the Main.

When he returned in 1860, the first intelligence that reached him after his arrival at his home, was that the entire capital of the Chicago Marine and Fire Insurance Company had been squandered by its responsible officers, during his absence.

He at once resumed its management, and endeavored to arrest still further disasters; but just then the Rebellion broke out, and the Southern Stocks, upon which the circulation of the Illinois banks was based, becoming nearly worthless, the whole banking system of the State went down. Mr. Scammon worked away resolutely, dealing equally and fairly by all his customers, and in a short time had paid off the indebtedness of the institution, which had been thus robbed and ruined. He restored capital and credit to the company, and under his management his institution continued to enjoy the public confidence, and to transact a large business, until the losses of the great fire and the panic of 1873 rendered it expedient to wind them up. He was always opposed to illegal and depreciated currency of the "wild-cat" order. The acts of the Legislature, which drove illegal currency from the State were written by him, and passed through his exertions. As a member of the Legislature of 1861, he obtained further stringent legislation on the subject of banking. At the time of the great fire he occupied an enviable position. He had won celebrity as a lawyer, and unlimited credit in business as a banker, and had become possessed of a vast fortune. But the terrible fire swept away his banks, warehouses, stores, and residence; fully half a million dollar's worth of property. In less than a week he had improvised a building on the site of his late residence and resumed his banking business. He was confident the city would be rebuilt, and the old landmarks restored. In fifteen months from the time of the fire, he had expended over a million dollars in rebuilding stores, warehouses, etc. He not only shouldered this enormous work, but he also assisted others to a large extent in their efforts to rebuild. Just in the midst of these gigantic undertakings occurred the defection of the *Chicago Tribune* from the cause of the Republican party, leaving that party without a representative morning paper in the city. Through all his eventful professional and business career he had never failed to take a deep and active interest in national politics, and had aided materially in establishing both of the Republican newspapers in Chicago. In view of this defection, and the approaching Presidential campaign, he decided to found a first-class metropolitan newspaper, that should be a powerful representative and advocate of the principles of the Republican party. He accordingly constructed a building in the rear of his residence, put in the necessary fixtures, engaged his editorial corps, and on March 25th, 1872, issued the first number of the *Inter Ocean*. This paper proved a success, and now has a larger weekly circulation than any other political paper west of the Alleghanies. The paper, outgrowing its limited accommodations, was removed to its present commodious quarters, 117 Lake St. But this enterprise brought upon him the most malignant and slanderous attacks from a rival press, which were followed up with such persistence and ferocity, as to injure both his individual credit, and that of the moneyed institutions with which he was connected. It remains to be said that, after the splendid success of a lifetime, Mr. Scammon has become seriously involved, in consequence of his great losses by fires, his immense expenditure in rebuilding, and the loans and assistance he rendered others who were rebuilding. He has suffered from four considerable conflagrations within the last four years; and, what is remarkable, his fine residence and surrounding buildings have been twice swept away; first in the great fire of 1871, and again in the great fire of July, 1874, and in both instances his premises were the last ones burned, while adjoining buildings, that were not so well protected, escaped unharmed.

He is now quietly engaged in the settlement of his affairs, and in the practice of his profession as a lawyer in Chicago. Many of the public institutions of the city owe their origin to him. He was one of the founders of the Chicago Academy of Sciences, and of the Chicago Astronomical Society. He was the first of the Swedenborgian or New Churchman in Chicago, and one of the original founders of the Illinois Association of that Church. He organized the Church of the New Jerusalem in Chicago. He was the first layman of prominence to favor the practice of homœopathy in Chicago, and built and conveyed free to the Hahnemann Homœopathic Society a commodious hospital. The Dearborn Tower of the edifice of the Chicago University, in which is placed one of the largest refracting telescopes in the world, was built at his expense, and the salary of its director paid by him till the great fire of 1871. On his return from Europe in 1860, he was elected one of the trustees of the University, and has been for many years Vice-President of its Board of Trustees, and the acting President of the same.

As a lawyer, banker, and editor, he has achieved distinguished success, and is a man of large literary and general culture. His private character has been one of moral and religious worth. Mr. Scammon is an industrious, energetic man, of robust constitution, and vigorously employing the powers which have in times past reaped wealth for him; and there is still prospect before him of years of honor, usefulness, and fortune. He bears on his shield the words *Confide in Domino.*

CHARLES WALKER, ESQ.

[From the Chicago Magazine, March, 1857.]

The subject of this sketch is a descendent of an old and wealthy English family of some note, who, in Cromwell's time, were portioned upon the Tweeds and called by the significant name of *Borderers;* members of which were among the earliest adventurers to this country, for we find mention made of his more immediate ancestors, as settlers in the Eastern part of New England, as early as 1640.

Col. William W. Walker, the father of Charles, was a native of Massachusetts. His father, who was a noted cattle dealer, at an early day moved his family to Ringe, New Hampshire, from which place Col. Walker emigrated at the age of 21, having little or no capital, save his trusty axe and that hardy education, which ever characterized the early sons of New England. Admiring the country of Central New York, he located in Plainfield, Otsego County, then but a wilderness. Here he became acquainted with a Miss Lucretia Ferrell, also a native of Massachusetts, whom he subsequently married, and with whom he lived upwards of fifty-five years. Though an Octogenarian, Col. Walker is still in the full enjoyment of all his faculties, having in his life-time filled many important political stations, been prominent and active in the church, ready to lend a help-hand to all worthy benevolent objects, and at the same time secured to himself a competence and the universal respect and esteem of his fellow-citizens.

Charles is the oldest son of William W. and Lucretia Walker, and was born February 2, 1802. The country being new, as we have before stated, his educational advantages were necessarily very limited. To a new log school-house, which a few enterprising farmers had built, the young lad was sent, at the early age of six years, to gain those elementary lessons, which have been turned to such practical account through a long life of usefulness. Inheriting a vigorous constitution, and withal an active and inquiring mind, together with uncommon diligence, he not only performed an unusual amount of manual labor upon his father's farm, but made most rapid progress in his studies. Improving his advantages to the utmost during three months in the year, he studied with his teacher during the day, and with his parents during the long winter evenings. Though as a boy

among boys in these juvenile days, his vigor of mind and decision of purpose was such, that notwithstanding his limited advantages, we find he was qualified for, and entered upon, the
duties of teacher at the early age of 15; and from that time forward continued in the same vocation during the winter months
until he attained his majority, with uncommon success. He
may well, we think, look back upon that era of his life, with
peculiar pride and pleasure, as he now recognizes the names of
many of his old pupils among the distinguished men, of the
East and West. While thus engaged, then 18 years of age, he
commenced the study of law, but soon found the sedentary
habits of that profession not suited to his temperament, with
the advice of his physicians he relinquished that idea and
turned his attention to more active pursuits; we next hear of
him riding through the country, during the summer months,
making purchases of sheep and cattle for his father.

At twenty-one, his health being then much impaired, he resolved to enter the mercantile business, and to that end hired
himself out to a friend as clerk for a short time, at the very
moderate salary of eight dollars per month. It did not, however, require a long clerkship for him to become a complete
master of that merchant's method of doing business, and in two
months he had fully determined to start in business for himself
the following spring.

In the spring of 1824, with $1350 aggregate capital, compiled
of $350 of his own private funds, $500 given him by his father,
being in fact his own earnings, and $500 loaned of a neighbor-
ing farmer, he started for the city of New York, with no letters
of credit, reference, or recommendation; and the following
May, opened his store upon the economical plan of doing his
own work, and soon after made his first purchase of grain. The
next spring, when he went East to make his purchases, he made
his first appearance at the Bull's Head Cattle Yard, New York,
where the Bowery Theatre now stands, with a fine drove of fat
cattle. By close and judicious management business prospered
till 1828. But shipping in the fall of that year a large amount
of cheese, butter, and pork, to a southern market, the cheese
became damaged at sea, and through the mismanagement of
agents, and the misapplication of funds, nearly all the accumulated fruits of four years laborious toil were swept away.

But by attending personally to the sales in New York, and
the purchases at home, business flourished till '32, when a sudden decline in the price of provisions occasioned another heavy
loss. But from 1833 to '34, large operations in all the leading
products, attended by a steady and gradual rise, brought to a
successful termination all his business operations. In the spring
of '33, being in New York, he accidently became a purchaser
from a cargo of raw hides from Buenos Ayres, which he was
enabled to obtain upon favorable terms; but upon getting them

home, and finding they were somewhat injured and could not be turned into the New York market without serious loss, he hit upon the expedient of manufacturing them into boots and shoes, and disposing of them at the fall Indian payments at Chicago; in the furtherance of which plan, his brother, Mr. Almond Walker, was in due time sent on, who opened his assorted stock of guns, boots, shoes, and leather, at Fort Dearborn, in the autumn of 1834.

By this adventure his attention was turned toward the West, where he soon saw and appreciated her undeveloped resources; and early the ensuing spring—not twenty-one years ago—he was on his way to this city, with ready means, enlarged and liberal views, an extensive business experience and acquaintance, in the vigor of manhood, with a widespread and favorable reputation at the East, to unite his fortunes with the destinies, and contribute his energies to the development of the unknown resources of this then lake shore village. Among his first operations here was the buying of several lots of real estate, among which was the purchase of John S. Wright, Esq., the corner of Clark and South Water Streets, in connection with Capt. Bigelow, of Boston, and Jones, King & Co., of Chicago, for the sum of $15,000, *cash;* which was considered by many at that time, a most visionary speculation. Some days subsequent to making this purchase, after reconnoitering in the country, he publicly avowed the then bold opinion that Chicago was destined to be the great city of the inland seas, and in test of his faith in this prediction, immediately set about making this city the principal point for his future operations. In May, '35, while on his way to Chicago, being detained at St. Josephs, there being no regular means of conveyance across the lake at that time, he made several purchases of hides from the flat boats and butchers' stalls for the Eastern market, to which were subsequently added purchases made in and about Chicago; this shipment, it is believed, is the first ever made from the State of Illinois to any point as far east as Utica or Albany.

The next year he established business in Chicago with the late E. B. Hurlburt, Esq., under the firm of "Walker & Co.," upon South Water street, for importing implements of husbandry and household utensils from the East, together with a store of general merchandise, taking in exchange the various products of the West. During this period he was much of the time riding through the country, on horseback, as far north as Green Bay, locating government lands at the Four Lakes (now Madison), Beloit, and other points on the Rock and Milwaukee Rivers.

The next year came the terrible financial revulsions of '37, when ruin and desolation swept the whole country, those who sat in the high places of wealth and affluence were drawn irresistably into the maelstrom of utter insolvency. Banks, like business men, came down with a crash, and the depreciation of currency produced ruinous confusion in the mediums of exchange. But Mr. Walker was one of the very few men, extensively engaged in business, who stood up against the storm; though he had to bring to bear his best energies and most expert financial skill, for maturing liabilities pressed hard upon him, and his name was largely endorsed upon the paper of other men; had not his reputation in Eastern commercial circles been of the best character, he would certainly have been swamped with thousands of others. But he found, in this emergency, that the relation he thus held as an important commercial medium between the merchant and artisan of the East, and the pioneer husbandman of the West, of immeasurable advantage. The extensive and favorable business reputation he enjoyed among the leading men and Banks of the East, as well as the confidence of the dealers of the West, enabled him to greatly enlarge his operations. To prevent the necessity of purchasing Eastern drafts at ruinous rates, he adopted the plan of purchasing the products of the country with the depreciated currency of the West, and made his extensive shipments of products the medium of exchange through which to meet his Eastern liabilities. Thus he was enabled to prevent the entire stagnation of business at home, preserve his reputation abroad, and in a few years of almost unprecedented vigilance and activity, to entirely overcome all his embarrassments.

The next year his firm purchased a few bags of grain of the surrounding farmers, which were sent to his mills in Otsego County, New York; this shipment of wheat, we believe, was the first ever made from Chicago to so Eastern a market.

During this period, though making Chicago the principal theatre of his labors, he was yet a resident of the State of New York, dividing his time nearly equally between this city, his home in Otsego County; New York City, and traveling on business. In '39, the famous struggle between the old Safety Fund, and the so-called Red Dog, or free banking system, was at its height. As a Representative from his native county he was sent to the Legislature. Carrying with him the same comprehensive and far-seeing views as a legislator, that ever characterized him as a business man, he was intrumental, in no small degree, in carrying through, though opposed by the great preponderance of the money power of the State, that deservedly popular system of redemption and exchange, which has since that time been in effect.

Each succeeding year his business in Chicago continued to increase, so that in 1840, his shipments had so much enlarged, that in the purchase of hides and skins alone, he not only exhausted his supply of merchandise, but was obliged to bring money from the East. In 1842, he established a partnership with Cyrus Clark, Esq., of Utica, under the firm of Walker &

Clark, for receiving Western produce; to bring himself nearer the chief point of business, he resolved to close out his affars in Otsego County, and in May, 1845, he removed his family to our city.

In 1847, came the great crisis in the grain trade which carried down the oldest and best houses in the Union. Though not escaping without some most terrible losses that would have intimidated ordinary men; with a courage undaunted by reverses—with a nerve and will, equal to the emergency, his craft was guided to a safe anchorage from the fearful breakers that engulped his less fortunate competitors; and his firm continued to hold its position as the leading grain and produce house in the West.

In 1851, it was found that C. Walker & Son of Chicago, Walker & Kellog of Peoria, and Walker & Clark of Buffalo, were the largest purchasers of grain from the farmers, in the United States. So that the few bags of grain, which in 1839 were sent on their eastern journey and the few bushels of 1840, had, in 1851, grown to 1,500,000 bushels.

At this period a severe attack of that malignant disease, the cholera, destroyed his health and compelled him to leave the financial management of the business to his oldest son, who continued the same under the firm of C. Walker & Son and C. Walker & Sons, till 1855, when he retired from the business altogether, leaving it to his two sons and others, who continue the same under the firm of Walker, Bronson & Co., prosecuting the business with all the vigor of its founder, this firm have during the past year, handled over *five and a quarter millions* of bushels of grain, an amount, we think, which will bear comparison with that of any other establishment in our own country or in Europe. Mr. Walker retires, we understand, the oldest grain merchant in the Union, having steadily remained in one of the most hazardous speculations in the world over thirty-one years. Acting upon the principle that he who can so cheapen and make efficient the avenues of trade, as to bring the productions of the country so much nearer a market, that the farmer can receive but one penny more the bushel for his grain, brings millions to his country, he feels amply repaid for the great risks he has run; and whatever benefit may have accrued to himself, that he has rendered an ample equivalent to those whom he has served.

While thus engaged as a pioneer in his own peculiar business he has been none the less efficient in promoting works of public utility. Prominent in all those great schemes which do so much towards developing the resources of the country, he has ever been one of the foremost in opening up and turning to account those great thoroughfares which vein our broad prairies, and wind their deep channels through our hills and valleys, and which, with every throb of animated industry, quicken into life new avenues of trade, turning their accumulated wealth to swell the commercial tide that has so strongly set to the heart of our western metropolis.

When the Galena Rail Road was recuscitated, in 1847, Mr. Walker was chosen one of its Directors. He entered into the project with all his heart. In its gloomiest days, his faith never faltered; his confidence in the ability of the country to build the road never failed. When it was found that more subscriptions were necessary, he, as one of a Committee for soliciting additional subscriptions, traversed the country westward, and as far north as Beloit. His courage never wavered. When, in its darkest days, at a meeting of the Board, all confidence seemed to have departed from a majority of the Directors, he, with two or three others, remained firm in his confidence that the work would go through without failure. "A Committee of the Believing" was appointed to take measures to prevent immediate disaster, composed of himself, J. Young Scammon, Esq , and one other. Their measures were successful; and when, on the return of its President, Mr. Ogden, from New York, it became necessary that the Directors should become individually liable for a large sum of money, to secure the iron to lay the first divison of the Road; Mr. Walker did not hesitate to be among the first to do so; and to the credit of the Board be it said, that all the Chicago Directors, but one, pledged their individual liability for the progress of the work. Mr. Walker remained in the Directory from the first, and took an active part in the construction and management of the Road.

In Feb., 1856, the enterprise of pushing forward, across Iowa, the counterpart of the Galena Railroad, was projected; and the Chicago, Iowa, and Nebraska Railroad was organized, having its eastern termination at the young and growing town of Clinton, on the western bank of the Mississippi. Of this Company Mr. Walker was one of the main directors and its president.

During the summer of 1856, he, in connection with others, erected and put in operation, at Beloit, Wis., an excellent paper mill, and a large reaper manufactory; and from a very superior quality of clay, upon his farm in Morris, Ill., commenced the manufacture of " Green Mountain Ware," expecting, in time, to supply Chicago and the Northwest with a quality of stoneware equal to any in the United States. He also was largely engaged in farming in the interior.

The conviction, that he who does the most towards opening up the great channels of trade, so that the poor man's labor will gain a level with the rich man's capital, is a practical philanthrophist, he was in theory and practice a thorough utilitarian. In private life, a plain man and thoroughly democratic; he recited the incidents of his boyhood and early struggles with a degree of well-earned satisfaction, and none more ready, in every consistant way, with kind words or material countenance

and aid, to cheer onward honest and persevering industry. From
the first, a faithful and influential member of the church, and a
most exemplary man, we think we do no injustice to any other
citizen to say, that while we are frank to concede there are
others who have added to themselves greater wealth, to none is
Chicago more indebted for her unexampled prosperity than to
the late Charles Walker.

In closing this brief notice of one so highly esteemed, we may
fitly add the words of another: "In the internal improvements,
which have done so much to develop the exhaustless resources
of the State, in Railroad enterprises, which have poured a flood-
tide of wealth and business into our commercial metropolis of
the Northwest, in every public work, whose intention and effect
was to build up and promote the healthful growth of the City,
he has ever been in the foremost rank of public-spirited men.
In short, taking into consideration the varied incidents of his
active life, his indomitable perseverance and industry, and the
financial ability he has exhibited, Mr. Charles Walker has had
few equals and no superiors, as a skilful business man and a
good citizen."

THOMAS CHURCH, ESQ.

By JAMES TAYLOR, Ph. D.

Author of "Moral and Social Manners," etc.

INTRODUCTION.

There is a laudable craving in the human heart, to know the history of those who have become distinguished, whether such distinction is the result of personal merit, or of the peculiar circumstances by which they are surrounded. It has been said, that "some are born great, some have greatness thrust upon them;" but certain it is that, however favorable circumstances may be, it requires an inherent power to seize, at the right moment, the advantages which time and circumstances may offer the enterprising and watchful. The life of Thomas Church furnishes interesting material, in connection with the early settlement of Chicago, and is a very prominent example of what may be accomplished by a steady perseverance in an honorable course of industry, integrity, and self-reliance.

The name of Thomas Church will ever be remembered with respect and affection by those who knew him best, and were able to appreciate the many estimable qualities which so well fitted him to take an active part in the early settlement of Chicago, with the interests of which he was identified from the year 1834, to the time of his death, on the 25th day of June, 1871.

The honorable and exemplary life of Thomas Church well deserves a record, which will hand his name to posterity, and keep green the memory of his many virtues, his goodness of heart, and noble aspirations.

On the front page of the "Family Bible," as is customary in rural homes, the record of the Church family was kept, from which it appears, that Thomas Church was born, in the Town and County of Onondago, in the State of New York, on the 8th day of December, A. D. 1800. His father died while Thomas was in his infancy. His mother's maiden name was Olive Rawson, who had been bereft of her husband, and afterwards, by a second marriage, became the wife of Thomas Yates, a man of moderate means, but industrious, enterprising, and honorable. In the household of his step-father, young Church was brought up. Mr. Yates was the owner of a distillery, and the boy, Thomas, was employed in such matters as his strength would permit him to perform. It was his business to carry, on horseback, the meal from the mill, and to assist in clearing a small farm, where they raised wheat for the family consumption. They had three cows, and a span of horses, with which, when the roads were passable, Mr. Yates used to do teaming, from Albany, for the neighboring merchants. The family were in good circumstances, compared with their neighbors. They were very temperate, for Thomas never new but of one pint of rum being sent for, and that was on account of sickness, except, on another occasion, when two quarts of whisky were purchased, when they had a 'logging bee.'

When Thomas was twelve years old, the father removed to the town of Benton, Ontario County. From this time he used to assist his mother, and, at times, went to school. He occasionally did little chores for the neighbors, for pay, and one day earned six and a-half cents, for gathering stones from a hay meadow. Small as were these earnings, he had a purse of his own, and was anxious to increase his store. When he was fourteen years of age, his parents removed to Bennington, Genesee County, on the border of civilization, and there he practiced a pioneer life, helping to clear, with his two younger brothers and his father, as much land as they were able. Here were spent five years, their home a log house, roofed with split-staves and bark, split and hewed logs for the floor, and stakes set in auger-holes, with a board on them for seats; a broad chimney, funnel-shaped, big end down, plastered within with clay and straw. The manufacture of maple sugar formed a part of their employment, and very much interrupted the attendance at school.

And now occurred one of those events which illustrate on what trifles our destinies depend. A disagreement between Thomas and his step-father took place, as to whether he should have the large or the small knife to cut basket wood. His father told him, that "unless you have everything your own way, you will not do anything." This charge was denied, and he was then told: "If he did not like to remain at home, he could leave." The young man replied: "If I thought you were in earnest, I would jump the bars as quick as you like." And upon this he let fall the axe, "jumped the bars," and left his home. That jump—from home into the world—was ever remembered as a mighty event.

And now, launched upon the world without knowing where to go—without money—without friends—with only the clothes he had on—no friends to aid or advise! His thoughts turned to those who were better off, who had the advantages of education, wealth, parents, kind friends that would help them. He envied those who had learned a profession or trade. He stood alone—without help—almost without hope! But he had health and youth, and as the first sadness wore away, hope revived, he felt stronger, and resolved that, with an honest purpose, and with the help of God, he would on himself rely; that he would take no step backward, and he hurried on to seek employment. About three miles from his home, he engaged to tend a mason for two weeks, for which he was to receive twelve bushels of wheat and six York shillings in money. The man he had worked for was a miller. There came to the mill a brother of young Church, with a grist. Thomas told him that he had twelve bushels of wheat, for which he could get only thirty-seven and a-half cents a bushel, but he wanted to help pay the clearing, and if his father would send his bags, he could have the wheat.

The boy soon came back with the bags and got the wheat; but young Church was afraid his father might relent; but he did not. The wheat was gone, and he now had a capital of six York shillings. However, he agreed to work for the same man, Mr. Owen Cotton, for one year, at ten dollars a month, the payment to be made as follows: fifteen dollars in cash, fifteen dollars in orders on a dry-goods store; half the balance in horn cattle, and the other half in grain, at barter price, *viz.*, fifty cents a bushel, the market price being thirty-seven and a-half cents. In this situation he learned to run a linseed oil mill, a grist mill, and a saw mill; and, as Mr. Cotton was often from home, young Church acted as clerk, sold lumber, grain, and oil, and often went with produce to the neighboring towns and exchanged it for raw material. Thus he gained some knowledge of trade, improved his education, and saw a little of the world. He had now made the acquaintance of Miss Rachel Warriner, and this inspired his ambition. Times improved, money became more plenty, and he exchanged his cattle and grain with Mr. Cotton for a little farm. He worked another year, during which time he sold the farm for cash; and, at the end of his term, he again agreed to work for six months for the sum of sixty dollars.

At the expiration of the two and a-half years, he had $227.00 in cash, and a new suit of clothes. Rachel waited, and, in 1823, they were married.

With new responsibilities, new plans were laid, and often thrown aside; but, ultimately, it was concluded to buy a small farm, and establish a home. With this view, Mr. Church went to Chatauque county, selected and bought a small piece of land, built a cabin on it, and then returned home on foot, by the way of Buffalo. There he was overtaken by a snow-storm, and detained one whole day. This delay was the cause of a radical change in all his plans.

Buffalo was then a village of 2500 inhabitants, and Mr. Church did not know any one. He had heard, however, of an acquaintance of his cousin, and this man he sought out. He found him keeping a little store, and as busy as a beaver, notwithstanding the bad weather. While sitting in the store, the idea occurred to him, Why cannot I do something of this kind? And this thought occupied him during the remaining walk home of thirty miles. Of course, his wife was consulted. Her advice was—"Go to Buffalo—if your heart is set upon this enterprise, it will be successful." To Buffalo accordingly they went, in February, 1824, leased a spot of ground, and erected on it a small store and dwelling. When a stock of goods had been laid in, their money was exhausted, and customers were anxiously looked for. The first sale amounted to three cents. A one dollar bill was presented, and taken, and ninety-seven cents in silver given in exchange. Woful to relate—the bill proved to be on a broken bank! This mishap was a source of much self-reproach, that he should have taken a young wife to a strange place, locked up all his means in a business he knew nothing about; and here was a pretty beginning.—He did not tell his wife for some time. A bank note detector was now purchased, and soon matters began to mend. The venture proved successful. Trade increased; and the first year Mr. Church cleared $200. This was probably one of the pleasantest years of his life. It was his first venture in business, and the first year of his married life. All things prospered with him; and he had good reason to look forward to a successful business career, and a happy domestic life.

They remained ten years, during that time the lot he had occupied had grown in value, from $150 to $4000. In fact, Buffalo had become a city, competition came in, and it was this suggested a removal further west.

In the spring of 1834, Mr. Church embarked with his effects on board of a small schooner, bound for Chicago. Ever since 1832, when Gen. Scott's army had returned from the Black Hawk war, reports had been circulating of the great fertility of the soil of Illinois, and of the advantages which Chicago would offer to the adventurous settler. Congress, too, had made an appropriation of land to the State for the purpose of constructing a canal from Chicago to the Illinois river.

Far-seeing men discerned in this great enterprise an unbroken chain of water communication between the Mississippi and the great lakes, a sure prognostic of the future development of Illinois, and a bright harbinger of the brilliant destiny in store for her. Mr. Church himself was not insensible to these great advantages, although he, in common with the early settlers of Chicago, had no idea of the rapidity of the future growth of the city. It was supposed, too, that Congress would soon make an appropriation for the improvement of the harbor at the mouth of the Chicago river.

The schooner on which Mr. Church had embarked, arrived at Chicago on the second day of June, 1834, and anchored about three-quarters of a mile outside of the mouth of the river. No vessel had as yet passed over the bar into the river. The passengers came ashore in boats, and landed their goods in the

same way. We may mention here, that the first vessel that
entered the Chicago river was the schooner Illinois, Capt. Pick-
ering. This adventurous officer succeeded in passing the bar
in safety in the fall of 1834. It was considered, as indeed
it was, quite a feat, and an epoch in the history of the State.
That night a jubilee was held in the cabin of the schooner, at
which plenty of champagne was drunk, toasts given, and
speeches made.

There were about four hundred people in Chicago on Mr.
Church's arrival, besides the garrison at Fort Dearborn, which
embraced 200 U. S. troops. The business of the place was all
done on Water street. Mr. Church endeavored to buy a lot
there, but was unsuccessful. The land called canal lands was
principally owned by the State. Individuals who owned lots
would not sell them. Individuals claiming the canal lands by
possession, designated their claim by having a stick of timber
or an old stove on it, and asked $500 or $600 for their right
of possession. But speculation in lands was not what Mr.
Church came to Chicago for. He desired to get into business,
and wished at least to own the property on which he lived.
He succeeded, finally, in purchasing two lots. Nos. 111 and
113 Lake street, for $250 each, and immediately erected a
store and dwelling house on the property, 20 by 40 feet, and
two stories high. There were few or no regularly traveled
streets in Chicago at that time. The travel from the Fort to
the branching of the river was along the river bank and on
some ridges that crossed ravines leading to the stream. Mr.
Church's store was the first one built in Chicago fronting on
Lake street. Mr. J. K. Botsford had built a store on Dearborn
street a little while before, the end of which reached to Lake
street:—but at that time there were not enough houses built
to give direction to Lake street. In building his house, Mr.
C.'s greatest difficulty was to get assistance enough. After buying a raft of timber in the river, he had to get it sawed by hand
into joists and rafters, in the same manner that ship-timber
is sawed. The frame being prepared, a derrick was rigged,
and the frame raised to its place by a pair of oxen. His weather
boards were brought from the Wabash country, by what were
called "prairie schooners;" wagons drawn by five or six yoke of
oxen. This *land voyage* occupied several days, the *crew* taking
their provisions with them, and camping out at night. After
selling out their cargo and part of their oxen at Chicago, they
would take on board a return load of salt, groceries, or dry
goods, and 'set sail' for home again. A great deal of Mr. Church's
early trading was done with the captains of these *prairie schooners.* They continued their trips till the march of civilization
rendered them no longer necessary.

In the spring of 1835, Mr. Church went to Buffalo for a stock
of goods. It took five days to get to Detroit by stage. Send-

ing his goods by lake, he returned by way of Detroit and Michigan City. There was no regular wagon road, and all vehicles ran along on the beach of the lake. It took two days to come from Michigan City to Chicago. There were fourteen passengers on this trip. A lady and two gentlemen rode on the top of a wagon loaded with baggage. The other eleven passengers walked on before. The lady was Mrs. JOHN S. C. HOGAN, wife of the then postmaster at Chicago. Her husband, and Mr. JOHN L. WILSON, afterwards Sheriff of Cook county, were also in the party.

On arriving home, Mr. Church found that his goods had got there before him. During his absence, James Whitlock, Esq., Register, and Col. E. D. Taylor, Receiver of the General Land Office, had been negotiating with his wife for the preparation of a building for the use of the office, and she had agreed with them that, on his return, Mr. Church would fit up and furnish two rooms, in the upper story of his store, for their purpose. He immediately hired the necessary assistance, and set about the fulfilment of the contract. The rooms were finished by the first day of June, 1835, and the land sales of that year immediately commenced. The attendance of buyers was very large and the bidding quite spirited. The purchasers stood out on Lake street in front of the land-office, and the constant tramping of such a crowd made the place very muddy. To obviate this, and to give the public a dry place to stand, Mr. Church caused a large quantity of gravel to be brought from the lake shore, and spread daily over the street. The receipts from the sales of land in two weeks were over half a million of dollars. Mr. Church's profits on the goods sold at the same time and for three weeks thereafter, five weeks in all, was $800. The next spring, Mr. Church built an addition to his store, making it one hundred and eighty by twenty feet, and replenished it with a fresh stock of goods. In the year 1838, his retail sales for cash amounted to over $41,000. That year, and the preceding, was a hard year with merchants generally. The great commercial smash up of 1837 had shaken the country to its remotest extremities, and even Chicago felt its disastrous effects.

There are some very interesting incidents connected with Mr. Church's early experience of merchandising in Chicago. In 1837, he purchased at one time seventy-five tons of goods, the freight on which, from New York to Buffalo alone, was $1100. Late in the fall of 1837, sugar was very scarce here, and Mr. Church went to St. Louis, bought a large quantity, and had it re packed in barrels. This was necessary, as it had to be transported in wagons from Ottawa here, and the roads being none of the best, there was some danger that the teamsters might get stuck in the sloughs. In case this accident should happen, they could roll the barrels to *terra firma*. This lot of sugar cost eight and three-fourth cents per pound in St. Louis, and it sold here at the rate of six pounds for a dollar. It was customary to buy everything by the dollar's worth. The smallest change in money was a half dime. Sixteen of these, or eight dimes, passed for a dollar.

It was about this time that a change took place in the business of Chicago. Instead of importing all articles of necessity, Chicago now began to export provisions. Chicago merchants, too, now began to give credit to dealers in the country, to buy their produce, to borrow money on warehouse receipts, and to appoint foreign agents to do their business for them. Mr. Church, however, did not engage in this branch of traffic, but added to his other importations, paints, glass, oils, iron, and domestic dry goods. In 1840, he moved his old store, and built a forty feet front, fire-proof brick building on Lake street, Nos. 111 and 113, and moved his goods into it, taking into partnership his best clerk, Mr. M. L. Satterlee, late of the firm of Satterlee, Cook & Co.

After a successful business of three years, Mr. Church bought out Mr. Satterlee, and this partnership was dissolved in 1843, when Mr. Church disposed of his interest in the store, and invested his means, which were now considerable, in the purchase of real estate. In his transactions in real estate, he was as fortunate as in his mercantile career. One of the predominant traits in his character, though not the ruling one, was caution. He was never disposed to embark in hazardous undertakings; but he has uniformly succeeded in whatever he has undertaken.

An estimate of Mr. Church's property, on retiring from merchandising, showed a clear value of $37,000, and this was the result of twenty years' prudent enterprise, during which time he never was embarrassed to meet his engagement, and has always paid one hundred cents on the dollar, and never had a law suit which required the argument of an attorney.

Mr. Church now invested his means in real estate, having gained, by experience, a knowledge of the rapid rise in value; and so successful were his investments that, in the year 1856, his interest and rents amounted to $10,000; and, in 1857, to double that amount. The property was estimated, January, 1857, at $300,000, and his income $22,554.50 per annum. The havoc of panics has rendered these estimates subject to great vicissitudes; but, like the receding wave of the flood-tide, the rise of the reflux exceeds the depression, and an advance is maintained.

The rise in the value of land in Chicago, commenced at an early day. In 1830 or 1831, twenty feet of ground on Lake st., west of, and adjoining No. 113, sold for $7. In 1834, the same ground was sold for $250. In 1836, it was sold for $8000, it having then a building on it not worth over $2000. It is now worth or $1500 per foot, the snug little sum of $30,000.

In June, 1836, the great Canal sale commenced, and a large

amount of canal lands were sold. The terms were, a quarter down, and the balance in one, two, and three years, with interest on the deferred payments at six per cent. in advance. That was all, however, that was ever paid, as a few years afterwards the State compromised with the purchasers, giving them one-half of the whole quantity of the land for the one-quarter of the price which they had paid. In 1838, the State offered their lands on twenty years time, ten per cent. of the purchase money down, and six per cent. interest for the balance. They took in payment, too, State Stock, which was then depreciated to such an extent that thirty dollars of it could be bought for ten dollars. Such an opportunity to invest money profitably in lands has never occurred since; but at that time nobody wanted to buy, for there was very little money in circulation. In 1839, at the Fort Dearborn sales, lots on Michigan avenue were purchased at a little over $1 per front foot, lots of 48 feet front selling at $51. The same lots are now worth forty thousand dollars. Since that date, land has been steadily increasing in value.

In the summer of 1834, the first Tremont House was built on the north-west corner of Lake and Dearborn streets. It was burned down in 1839, that being the first large fire that had ever happened in Chicago. Mr. Ira Couch immediately built the second Tremont House on the site of the present edifice, and kept it till it too, was burned down in 1849. In the fall of 1849, Mr. Couch erected another noble structure. It was called by the croakers at first "Couch's folly" in derision, some persons thinking it much too large for a place like Chicago. But immense as it is, it has been thronged with guests, and its popularity is increasing every year. In 1871, the Tremont House was again ravaged by the flames, and is again rebuilt in a style still more magnificent.

Mr. Church, notwithstanding his close attention to business, his active mind and benevolent disposition has always led him to the discharge of his duty as a citizen; active in the promotion of whatever would benefit the interests of Chicago, he felt a pride in its rapid progress. For eight or nine years, Mr. Church was city assessor of the south division, and also Commissioner for the opening of streets and alleys, for the partition of real estate, and in awarding widow's dower; for the planking and paving of streets, and for appraising the damages and benefits arising from the establishment of lines of wharfage and dockage on the river. In the entire course of his official conduct, requiring the making of maps of subdivisions of the city, and placing the abstract titles on record, we have not heard of a single mistake, or a single complaint of unfairness or partiality.

In 1849, Mr. Church was nominated for mayor of the City of Chicago, by the Whig party, but was defeated.

On the organization of the Fireman's Insurance Company, Mr. Church was elected president, and filled the office with great credit, commanding the respect and esteem of his brother directors. As a token of their respect, in 1863, they presented Mr. Church with a handsome gold watch; value, $250. The character of Mr. Church is too well known to require eulogy, but the object of a biographical sketch is to hand down to posterity the record he has made with his cotempories.

In 1854, when the cholera raged in our midst with such alarming fatality—when the angel of death held high revel in our streets—when strong men and little children alike were stricken down on every side—when medical skill and the tenderest care were unavailing to stay the progress of the plague or to snatch its victims from its deadly grasp—when all business was paralyzed and when hundreds were fleeing from the pestilence, Mr. Church remained at home, discharged his usual duties, and ministered to the wants of the sick around him. He was not alone in this. Many others of our citizens, like him, devoted themselves to the noble work of alleviating the sufferings they could not prevent.

Successful in his pecuniary circumstances, Mr. Church was not less prosperous in his domestic relations. He was happy in his first marriage, in the possession of the choice of his heart's first affections; in whom he found a congenial help in his early struggles, and a companion in his early successes. To her was born five children, two of whom survive and are married to very estimable gentlemen now living in Chicago. In April, 1839, Mrs. Church died, which was the cause of great affliction to her husband and family. His two children were deprived of a mother's fostering care, and his happy home had become desolate. Hired help can not supply the place of parental affection, and, for a time, there was sorrow in that dwelling.

In the fall of the same year, at the sick-bed of a neighbor, Mr. Church accidentally met Mrs. Rebecca Pruyne; knowing that she had no other interest than a neighborly sympathy, he thought it a manifestation of a kind heart, and became favorably impressed. She was a lady of comely appearance, respectably connected, was the widow of the late Peter Pruyne. Mr. Pruyne was senator of this State, and Rebecca was daughter of S. W. Sherman, of this city. She had one child. Mr. Church had two children; it was a legal proportion, she was entitled to her thirds. This casual meeting ripened into an acquaintance, and, ultimately, into a mutual sympathy and attachment, and, in November, 1839, they were married. The alliance proved mutually satisfactory, and, as their pecuniary circumstances were ample for their moderate habits, they had only to seek happiness in the rational enjoyments suited to their tastes. Their quiet of home life, they diversified by travel; they visited the homes of their early youth, and gratified themselves in again

viewing the scenes with which their affections and memories
were entwined. These travels were extended to many places
of interest. Mr. Church was, in the meantime, carrying on his
enterprises in real estate, building largely, and watching with
great interest the progress of the city, until June, 1871, when,
after a short illness, he died, regretted by a large circle of
friends. Obituary notices were published in the daily press,
and the directors of the Firemen's Insurance Company passed
the following resolutions:

Resolved—That the news of the death, on Sunday evening,
of our first and only president, Thomas Church, fills our hearts
with sorrow, and is an event greatly to be deplored.

Resolved—That his death is not only a loss to this company,
but to the community in which he has so long honorably and
exemplarily lived.

Resolved—That we will, in a body, attend his funeral, and
that we extend to his family our sympathies, and that these
resolutions be spread upon the records of the company, of which
he has so long been an honored and useful president.

Mr. Church was a large and fine looking man, of plain and un-
affected manners, and modest and retiring in his deportment.
We are not informed whether or not he was connected with any
religious society, but from our personal knowledge of his character, we should pronounce him to be Christian at heart and in
practice, whether he was so in name or not. He was one of our
wealthiest citizens, but he was esteemed and respected far more
for his estimable qualities, for his sound good sense, for his
active usefulness, and for his quiet and unostentatious benevolence, than for the adventitious glare of mere wealth.

Although part of the present sketch was in type before it was
submitted to the present editor, he has been permitted a sight
of an autobiography of the late Thomas Church. It is replete
with very interesting matter bearing upon the history of Chicago during nearly forty years of close observation. These
observations will form invaluable material in preparing a history of Chicago, but are too lengthy to be even glanced at in
this sketch we extract the following: "I feel very grateful and
thank a divine Providence for the good and kind husbands that
our daughters have. They are thrifty, industrious, and good
providers for their families. The eldest, Geo. A. Ingalls, is a
lawyer; the second, Ephram Ingals, is a doctor; the youngest,
S. D. Kimbark, is an iron merchant. Neither of them use pro-
fane language, or tobacco, and are quite temperate.. They all
came home last Thanksgiving-day, each brought their eldest
child, and I believe the arrangement is, that on next Thanksgiving-day, our extension-table is to be spread so as to admit
three more little ones. I feel proud of our boys, and have reason
to hope that they will continue in well-doing; remain good
men, good husbands, and good fathers!"

HON. WILLIAM H. BROWN.

By R. W. PATTERSON, D. D.

THE present writer has been requested to add to the fore-going sketch of Mr. Brown's life such facts as may be within his knowledge. Being obliged to depend solely on his own memory, he cannot hope to give such interesting particulars as may probably be known to other parties.

During the financial troubles of 1857-1860, Mr. Brown care-fully managed his affairs, and escaped serious embarrassment, having, as usual, kept out of debt, and taken good care of his property. In the year 1860, he was elected a member of the House of Representatives in the State Legislature. In this po-sition he acquitted himself honorably and usefully, being among the most industrious, judicious, and influential members of the body.

In the great struggle for the preservation of our government, which may be said to have commenced in a decided form in 1856, and which culminated in the memorable rebellion in 1861, Mr. Brown, as might have been expected, was deeply en-listed for the cause of liberty and the Union. During the Presidential canvass of 1860, he took an active part in support of Mr. Lincoln, and was as much elated, perhaps, as any man by the success of the Republicans. When, however, the rebellion of the Southern States became a certain fact, and internal war was inevitable, he was very much depressed, feeling, as he often said to the writer, that no one could predict the end. But he had faith in God, and had no doubt that it was the duty of every good citizen to stand for the defence of the right and the support of good government at whatever sacrifice. He cheer-

I a

fully paid his taxes to the Government, incurred by the war, and gave up his sons to the service of his country without a murmur.

After the war, as age was advancing upon him, Mr. Brown retired, in part, from business; devoting himself, chiefly, to the management of his own property. But he never lost his interest in the public welfare, and never gave up his positions in the several Boards of trust with which he was connected, such as those of the Chicago Orphan Asylum, and the Insane Asylum at Jacksonville. He continued to be active and faithful as a member and an elder of the Second Presbyterian Church until his departure for Europe, shortly before his death. He several times represented the Presbytery of Chicago in the General Assembly as a Ruling Elder, and was widely known in the denomination as among the most reliable friends of its enterprises. For many years, he was a corporate member of the American Board of Commissioners for Foreign Missions, to whose funds he was a large contributor during his life, and by a handsome provision in his will. And the cause of Home Missions had few, if any, more generous helpers. He was deeply interested, also, during all his later years, in the Mission Sunday School work, and in the Bethel cause, while in his own particular church he was always among the foremost givers, and the most devoted and steadfast supporters, being uniformly in his place on the Sabbath and in the weekly prayer meeting, as well as on special occasions.

In the summer of the year 1866, Mr. and Mrs. Brown left Chicago on a tour to Europe, partly for pleasure and partly on account of his failing health. During this trip, his keen relish for new scenes, and his habit of activity, led him to exert himself beyond his strength. After traveling through Great Britain and extensively through the countries of Europe, he occasionally exhibited signs of exhaustion, and in Amsterdam, Holland, he was taken with the small-pox. When he seemed almost recovered from this distressing disease, and was preparing to resume his travels, he was suddenly seized with paralysis, and shortly sank under it, dying peacefully on the 17th of June, 1867, at the age of 72 years. In the early part of August, following, the writer visited the old Bible House and the room in which Mr. Brown's spirit took its flight, went to his grave, and saw the coffin that contained all of him that was mortal.

In the autumn of that year, his remains were transferred to their final resting-place in Graceland Cemetery.

His widow, Mrs. Harriet C. Brown; his four sons, S. Lockwood, Charles B., Theodore F., and Frederick, and his daughter, Mrs. Mary Tyler, survive him, and are still residents of Chicago.

I trust I shall be pardoned if I now add some of my own personal recollections and impressions of Mr. Brown, as I knew him in his public and private relations.

It was my privilege to become acquainted with Mr. Brown in the year 1833, when I was a student in Illinois College, although I had known him, by reputation, for a considerable time before. For he was a prominent citizen of this State almost from its admission into the Union, having become a citizen in the Territory while he was yet a very young man, and having risen to a position of distinction and public usefulness before he had reached the age of twenty-five years. Being, when I first saw him, among the more noted friends of church music in the State, he was invited to attend a musical convention at Jacksonville, which was held immediately after the annual commencement in the College. In this way I was first drawn to him as being interested in a subject that always engrossed a share of my own thought and attention. After that occasion, I kept up a knowledge of his movements until the year 1840, when I met him again in Chicago, where he had already resided for some years, and was an officer in the First Presbyterian Church. During the summer of that year, I learned more of his personal traits and peculiarities than I had known before, and was more than ever attracted to him. From that time onward until his death, I knew him intimately as a friend and as an Elder in the church of which I was Pastor from its organization in 1842, till the year 1873, six years after his decease in Europe. It will thus be seen that I had an opportunity of special acquaintance with Mr. Brown, such as few others enjoyed. And still cherishing his memory with the warmest regard, I take pleasure in adding this small contribution to the memorial of him, which it is the desire of his family and friends to put on permanent record in this volume.

I have known well and long many of Mr. Brown's attached friends, among whom were Joseph Eccles, Esq., of Hillsborough, Hon. Samuel D. Lockwood, formerly of Jacksonville, and who died two years ago at Batavia; Hon. Thos. Mather, Hon. John T. Stuart, John Todd, M.D., and Rev. John G. Bergen, D. D., of Springfield; President Abraham Lincoln; Rev. William K. Stewart, of Vandalia; and Rev. Thuron Baldwin, D.D., late of New Jersey. A man who commanded the confidence of such gentlemen must have possessed excellences of no ordinary class. Especially deserving of mention was the life-long intimacy between him and Judge Lockwood, one of the purest and noblest men Illinois ever numbered among her jurists and citizens. Only a year before Judge Lockwood's death, in conversation with the writer, he referred in the most affectionate terms to his lamented friend, Mr. Brown, whom he was accustomed to visit every month during all the later years of his life. I well remember the estimation in which Mr. Brown was held by the older citizens of the State—lawyers, physicians, clergymen, and others, such as Judge Pope, Benj. Mills, Esq., Dr. Newhall, Hon. David A. Smith, and Rev. John M. Peck, D.D.

Among the notable traits of Mr. Brown's character were the following:

1. He was fair and conscientious in his political commitments and action. He was decided in his convictions, first as a Whig and then as a Republican, but never did I know or hear of his espousing the cause of a notoriously bad man of his own party. He may on some occasions have quietly voted for one man of questionable character, but of good principles, in preference to another worse man whose principles he deemed erroneous and mischievous. But he never warmly supported a corrupt man of any party. And he always urged the nomination of good men. He was not a political partisan, but a true, generous patriot.

2. Mr. Brown was a sincere philanthropist. He abhorred those levelling ideas of equality that would destroy all the rights of property, and break up family and social ties as established at present in civilized communities. But he earnestly

contended for individual and political liberty, and while he
never favored what seemed to him impracticable schemes for
the emancipation of the enslaved, he firmly resisted the efforts
that were made for the introduction of slavery into this State,
and did more, perhaps, than any other 'man to avert that great
curse from Illinois, when parties were nearly equally balanced;
thus saving the State for the cause of freedom—an event, that,
in its consequences, probably turned the scale in favor of our
national government in the recent bloody strife between the
North and the South. Mr. Brown was not a sentimental philanthropist; he carefully inquired how he could do the most for
humanity at large, instead of yielding to every momentary impulse on the presentation of distress. Thus he co-operated
with every well-devised endeavor to provide for the needy and
the suffering, while he sometimes turned away the improvident
beggar. He was a foremost friend of orphan asylums, hospitals,
and other kindred institutions established by the State or by
private beneficence, doing always his full share to help them.
He was philanthropic on principle, and not from mere impulse.

3. He was, in general, a liberal and useful member of society.
He gave generously to every cause that commended itself to his
judgment, while at times he firmly rejected applications that
seemed to him unworthy of patronage. It would be difficult to
name a good enterprise begun in Chicago, during his residence
in the city, for which he did not contribute. And he was an
active helper in a great number of patriotic endeavors. I used
to think there was scarcely another man in Chicago whose name
was found high up on more subscription papers, or who was a
member of more committees and boards organized for benefi-
cent purposes.

4. Mr. Brown was scrupulously honest and trustful in every
relation of life. I never knew him to be accused of unfairness
or deception in any business transaction. I never heard a sus-
picion breathed against his integrity. I never met with a person who ventured to charge him with untruthfulness or prevari-
cation. He always seemed to me unusually fair and candid in
his statements of facts. I am sure I express the judgment of
all those who knew him best when I say that he was extraordi-
narily exact in his adherence to the requirements of truth and

justice, both in speech and conduct. This would hardly have been denied by his bitterest enemy.

5. He was naturally conservative, but never seemed to regard public opinion, when his duty required him to assume unpopular ground. He never betrayed any cause to which he had pledged his support, however misrepresented and misunderstood it may have become. And yet he was open to conviction in regard to the wisdom of any measure that he might have formerly sustained or refused to further by his money or personal influence. He was not vacillating in his judgments, for he usually considered every subject carefully before he formed his opinions respecting it. But I always expected to obtain a fair hearing when I undertook to present reasons for any view of a subject which I knew he did not favor; and in several instances he changed his grounds sooner than I had hoped for. In business matters, he was, perhaps, too conservative for such a city as Chicago; but, on the whole, his slowness to fall in with the prevailing estimates of property was, it may be, a good safeguard to his financial interests, and it tended to moderate the enthusiasm of the speculative spirit in times of dangerous inflation. Had he lived, he would, no doubt, have passed through this present trying crisis without disaster to his private fortunes.

6. Though not a man of brilliant mental powers, Mr. Brown was possessed of excellent practical judgment. He was not liberally educated, but he was not ignorant of books, and knew much more of the world than most men of more varied learning. His opinion in regard to matters of Church, State, or business, was always worthy of consideration. In fact, he seldom made a great mistake. I relied on his practical judgment, especially in trying situations, as on that of few other men; for he was scarcely ever carried away by temporary excitement, and he never lost sight of the main interests involved in any question, personal or public. Hence his counsel was often sought in relation to practical difficulties, both in church and in private affairs.

7. He was a most agreeable gentleman in social intercourse, and was warmly regarded as a personal friend. Those who knew him only slightly had but little idea of his power of

imparting interest to a social circle. His conversation was always entertaining, and hence his presence was sought and valued in general society. His house was the favorite resort of many gentlemen and families, who were attracted by his generous hospitality and the cordiality of his excellent lady.

As a friend, Mr. Brown could be safely trusted in all emergencies. He never flattered, and at times seemed cold and unsympathetic; but in the season of need he was uniformly a ready helper, and he could be relied on to speak kindly of you behind your back, if he professed friendship to your face. He could disagree with you without any breach of friendship. For he knew how to distinguish between great and little things. I sometimes thought it my duty to dissent from his opinion and to contend with him in regard to points of difference. But I could never see that it made any change in his subsequent deportment towards me. As a friend he was not demonstrative, but he was eminently true.

8. Mr. Brown was a man of positive opinions in regard to the character of others, but his judgments were, on the whole, charitable. He sometimes spoke severely of others, but not without apparent reason. He was, for the most part, careful in his utterances respecting his neighbors, and if he said anything unfavorable, it was usually qualified by some kinder expression. He was, by no means, guilty of double-dealing in his intercourse with men. If he was not always exactly tender of the reputation of others, he was usually reserved in the expression of adverse judgments, and almost uniformly he spoke kindly and commendingly of his neighbors and fellow-citizens. He was not a mischief-maker, and frequently merited the name of a peace-maker.

9. From intimate knowledge of Mr. Brown's principles, convictions, feelings, and conduct in a great variety of relations, I can truly say that I believe him to have been a sincerely and thoroughly *Christian* man. His religion was not impulsive, and he made no loud professions of zeal and spirituality. But I was always impressed with his evident depth of conviction in regard to the truth and claims of the Gospel, the purity of his Christian aims, the honesty and simplicity of his devotions, and his unfeigned and practical consecration to the service of the

Church and of his Lord. Few men have led more consistent Christian lives. His dying breath was one of prayer, and undoubtedly " he entered heaven with prayer."

In all that has been said, it has not been designed to assert or imply that Mr. Brown was, in the ordinary sense, a popular man. He had a certain severity of manner, in his intercourse with strangers, and sometimes with friends, that caused him to be misunderstood and misjudged. He did not sufficiently study the amenities of life, and he paid the temporal penalty of this neglect. Contrary to the common rule, he was most esteemed and loved by those who best knew his inner life. It was necessary to get through the outer shell to the real man to appreciate the nobleness of his character. Those persons who did this, will fully justify all that I have said of him.

Mr. Brown's memory will be blessed, not only by his own family, but by many friends, who felt, when he died, that a good and really great man had fallen, and who will keep his virtues embalmed in their hearts, when the blander traits of many more pliant men who were more widely applauded in life will be forgotten.

www.ingramcontent.com/pod-product-compliance
Lightning Source LLC
Chambersburg PA
CBHW051722090426
42738CB00010B/2038